Marketing
for Managers

Marketing for Managers

David Mercer

ORION
BUSINESS
BOOKS

The right of David Mercer to be identified as the
author of this work has been asserted by him in accordance with the
Copyright, Designs and Patents Act 1988

First published in Great Britain in 1998 by
Orion Business
An imprint of The Orion Publishing Group Ltd
Orion House, 5 Upper St Martin's Lane, London WC2H 9EA

A CIP catalogue record for this book
is available from the British Library

ISBN 0–75281–382–X

Typeset by Deltatype Ltd, Birkenhead, Merseyside
Printed in Great Britain by
Clays Ltd, St Ives plc

Contents

Chapter 1
The philosophy of marketing

Welcome, and thank you for giving up your time to read this book. In return, I will try to ensure that – by the time you have finished it – you will find that your investment of time is fully rewarded. As you are my 'customer', it is as important to me as it is to you that I succeed. For, if I don't succeed, you will not be a *satisfied* customer and will not buy any of my other books. Even worse, you will not recommend your friends to buy them. Indeed, if you are very dissatisfied, you will almost certainly go out of your way to persuade your friends and colleagues *not* to buy my books, and so I will have lost not just your business but that of perhaps ten more potential customers! I hope you can already begin to see why it is so important to develop satisfied customers and to invest in marketing.

As I can't, unfortunately, ask you personally why you have chosen this book to read, and certainly can't then write the book that would exactly meet those requirements, let me start by telling you what I hope the book will do for you – and, if this is not what you want, you can put the book down and move on to one that better meets your needs.

This book is designed for managers and professionals in general, not for marketing practitioners. It is for 'ordinary' mortals who only come into contact with marketing from time to time but still want to understand the strange language that its practitioners use in order to make some sense of conversations with them. It is for those of you who want to know why marketing is so important for the success of organisations, and want to understand something of how successful organisation make best use of it. Finally, it is so you yourself can use some of the ideas herein to improve your own performance as a manager or professional.

Just to make certain that you do fully understand, let me repeat that it is *not* for marketing practitioners. If are one of these, you should read my book *New Marketing Practice* (Penguin, 1997), which provides the detailed practical support you need. Neither is it for students on management courses; my own textbook *Marketing* (second edition, Blackwell, 1997), or that co-authored for the US market with Czinkotta and Kotabe (Blackwell, 1997), should provide the necessary level of academic theory you need to pass your exams! This book is for the great majority of practising managers and professionals, who are not directly involved in the marketing function but who – unknowingly – provide most of the real marketing support for their organisations. If you are in this latter category, then *please keep on reading*. If you are in the former categories, please put it down immediately and choose something more suitable!

Activity 1.1

I have said that one aim of the book is to generate ideas you can use in your own work. To help this process along, I will regularly suggest related 'activities' – exercises for you to carry out. These activities are included in order to give more practical meaning to the concepts I am describing by putting them into the context of what actually happens in your own organisation in general, and within the department or group (the more general term I will use from now on) with which you work.

But, here, the first question is a personal one: do you fit into the (latter) category of readers who, I think, will benefit most from reading this book? If the answer is 'yes', then welcome once more. If the answer is 'no', but you still want to continue (for I cannot ban you from reading it!), then please take a minute to jot down why so that you will be able to put the rest of your reading into a slightly different context from the one I am setting.

The foregoing nicely illustrates one of the most important (counter-intuitive) lessons of marketing, and that is the need to positively reject some business. If you haven't the right product or service for a customer, then withdraw. Carrying on, with the wrong offering, wastes both your own time and that of the customer and will lose you the goodwill for later sales that you might expect to win – whereas admitting your limitations builds the trust that will help you later. And another little recognised fact of marketing life is that it is usually those later sales that make all the effort worthwhile; it is very unusual to make a profit on your first sale (especially if it is to be the only one).

Activity 1.2

What do you think we mean by the term 'marketing'?

➡ WHAT IS MARKETING?

Surprisingly, in view of all that has been said and written on the subject, this is not an easy question to answer. In my academic textbook, addressing this question takes the first 30 pages – and even then I am not able to provide one simple answer. For 'marketing' means many different things to many different people. At one extreme, for instance, it is a *philosophy* that claims the customer should be at the focus of all you do, not least at the centre of all your strategic decisions. This outlook has been adopted by many corporations claiming to be very successful as a result, so it must mean something worthwhile to them and we will examine this aspect hereafter in this chapter. At the other extreme it is a *function*, a department or group within an organisation, to which marketing professionals are willing to dedicate their working lives – so it must also mean something to them. And it is, of course, also the *theories and techniques* of advertising, market research, sales and promotion, which rule the working lives of some marketing professionals and which are used by a marketing department to influence the buying behaviour of the organisation's customers. We will look at these latter aspects through the rest of the book.

The two aspects, philosophy and function, should perhaps be complementary; but they can often come up with very different solutions. Thus, I spent some years as a brand manager in part of

American Tobacco, where the whole focus of operations was determined by what marketing activities we – operating as a key marketing (department) *function* within the company – set in place. Later, I held a general management role in IBM, where everyone across the organisation contributed to its key marketing *philosophy* of 'customer service'. Both of these approaches worked – very successfully but very differently.

➡ THE PHILOSOPHY OF MARKETING

So, starting as I promised – and as a good marketer I always live up to my promises – let's have a look at the philosophy. It is, as I indicated earlier, a philosophy that puts the customer at the focus of everything the organisation does, not least at the centre of its strategies. This is very easy to say; indeed, it is a claim that almost all organisations would make. Only a few, in the public sector, would now insist that they rather than their clients know best; and even they, in their own way, are trying to help their clients. The problem is that, while it is easy to make the claim, it is much more difficult to do anything about it – and most organisations stumble at this point.

As we have seen, it is even difficult to decide exactly what marketing is. Even more problematical, therefore, is what a commitment to putting the customer at the focus of business really means. Unfortunately, for most organisations it seems to mean, in very general terms, that they just (barely) recognise that they need someone (anyone!) to buy their product or service. This is, I suppose, better than those organisations that see their customers as sheep to be 'fleeced', but just avoiding that pitfall is nothing like enough. If you really want to justify the claim that you are genuinely committed to a philosophy of marketing, you must start all your activities with the customer as the focus. You must then understand what a customer needs and wants; and your prime objective (even ahead of making a profit!) must be to meet those as best you can – and as the customer wishes.

In fact this, too, is unrealistic because it is a counsel of perfection. Most organisations do not have the abilities, or resources, to *exactly* meet every one of their customers' needs – let alone their wants! Most suppliers have a limited set of products and/or services, and a limited set of skills ('core competences' in the jargon of management), and they have to work within these. So there has to be some sort of compromise. The test of good marketing, in this context, is that it looks to the customer first and then to the organisation's limitations second, rather than the other way around.

Perhaps the best 'philosophical' approach is to persuade everyone across the organisation to put the customer first. This sounds impossibly idealistic, but it was the main marketing strategy adopted by IBM at the time when it was so successful. Its key organisational philosophy, one of only three that drove the company and all who worked in it, was 'customer service'. This applied to everyone, from the telephone operators at head office to the workers on the assembly lines in the factories – just as much as to the sales force. Whatever you were doing, you had only one criterion: will this give the best customer service? It was simple, and actually sounds rather simplistic, but it was incredibly powerful in practice. Not least, you never had to worry if you were following company policy; there was only one such policy, and most times it was obvious whether or not what you were doing was in the customer's best interests. That is the best example, and indeed definition, that I can give of what I mean by a genuine *philosophy* of marketing!

It is, though, a long way from what most people think of as marketing. It does not demand charismatic selling skills, or creative advertising, or even good market research. It is an attitude of mind. It simply asks that you do your best to help the customer – something most people would like to do anyway. We all get a good feeling when we help others, so isn't it nice that this is also the best form of marketing!

Activity 1.3

Taking your organisation as a whole, what do you think its marketing philosophy is? And is that the same as the management claim it is?

Taking your own group (department), what is your own marketing philosophy with regard to your own (internal?) customers – to those within the organisation you provide services for or work with?

➡ SELLING OR MARKETING?

My IBM example leads into a debate that was prevalent a few decades ago when 'marketing' was in its youth. The question then was, 'What are the differences between sales and marketing?' The answer, in crude form, was that as a sales team you sold what you had produced, using your skills to persuade the customers to take what you had to offer, or as a marketing department you found out what the customer wanted and produced that – the very reverse. It is said that the debate has long since ended; everyone now knows that marketing is the best approach. Yet the reality on the ground is less clear, and an understanding of the two approaches can help you understand some of the tensions that still arise.

The debate, it turned out, had little to do with what constituted good selling or good marketing. The best sales departments conducted superb marketing campaigns. IBM, for instance, used to send in teams of sales personnel to spend months surveying their largest customers – to find out exactly what those customers needed – and then it tailor-made the solution to exactly match those needs. IBM, in fact, thought it was selling, but it was really conducting near-perfect marketing. On the other hand, many advertisers have used extremely sophisticated techniques to sell things their potential customers didn't want. The classic example, from many years ago, was the Strand cigarette, which used incredibly creative commercials to put over the message that 'you're never alone with a Strand'. The problem was that the customers didn't even want to think about being alone!

To reiterate the point, this difference is not between functions within an organisation. Indeed, the sales function should be just as marketing-oriented as the marketing department – which is just as well since, despite the image portrayed by the media, most marketing is actually carried out, face-to-face, by sales personnel. At one extreme this is seen in the retail environment, where everybody coming into contact with the customer has a sales role – the checkout operators just as much as designated sales assistants – and this is especially true in those outlets offering services, such as banks and hairdressers. Similarly, many of those in the public services – librarians through to nurses – have much the same responsibilities for marketing in their own roles; indeed they are said to have a *vocation* for helping their 'customers'. Although they rarely describe this vocation in terms of customer service, their 'caring' approach once more represents more near-perfect marketing! At the other extreme, face-to-face marketing is seen in those industrial companies selling capital equipment, where teams of sales people may work on just one tender for literally years.

Unlike most other marketing books, which tend to highlight the advertising of consumer goods, I will therefore try to use *sales activities* as my main models, partly because it is easier to explain the concepts in such practical terms, partly because it is likely that these will be the focus of your own organisation's marketing activities, and partly because you should be able to identify a wider range of practical elements that you can yourself use. After all, you are probably not going to launch into your own mega-advertising campaigns! Indeed, the days when the stereotypical 'cowboy' salesman went out to persuade the poor 'prospect' to buy something he didn't want are largely a matter of history. Now it is all 'relationship management': investing in the long-term, so that the customer learns to trust you. There is only one way of doing that: showing the customer time after time that you really are trustworthy!

Activity 1.4

Almost certainly, your organisation will claim it has a marketing philosophy. But is this really true?

How about your own group? What notice do you take of your own (internal) customers?

➡ CO-OPERATION OR COMPETITION?

Relationship marketing was initially, in many respects, a reaction against the very aggressive policy of 'competition' promoted by many consultants and academics in the 1980s. At that time, when the Cold War was coming to an end, governments in the West placed great emphasis on 'the market' as a place where suppliers fought battles against each other – much as gunslingers did in Westerns. It might have been significant that the then US President learned his trade in precisely those films! What the politicians forgot was that 'the market' was invented to allow people to *co-operate*. What the suppliers often forgot was that not merely should they focus on customers, but they should co-operate with them. That is not to say that competitors should be ignored; you would be a foolish manager if you were not well aware of what your competitors were doing and didn't respond to their activities. But, above all, you should want to be better than them, to be best of all in serving the customer, to win the business. And you will put yourself in the best position to become best if you work *with* your customers rather than against them.

Surprisingly, it is also true if you work with your *competitors*, at least in terms of what is best for your industry. The Japanese, who seem to excel in most aspects of business, have just about the most ruthless competition between companies anywhere on Earth; but at the same time they work far more closely together with those same competitors to further the position of the industry they share – not least against less effective marketers in the West! But this is not just another aspect of Eastern deviousness, for something like it operates in the West too, but Westeners don't like to talk about it. My research shows that *most* companies co-operate with their competitors. And if they do so with their competitors, they surely do so with their customers, exactly as they should!

The essence of marketing, then, is co-operation with your customers – to best meet their wants and needs. The bonus, which almost always comes along, is that this usually also optimises your own organisation's performance (financial or otherwise); and helping your customers may also give you a warm feeling inside. The question, therefore, is not 'What can I sell you?' but 'How can I help you?' It is a shame that sales assistants are now persuaded *not* to say 'Can I help you?' – albeit that 'How can I help you?' is better since it does not generate the almost automatic response of 'No!' – but even with its shortcomings the traditional phrase encapsulates the most important aspect of the job: helping the customer.

In your own case, most likely working within an organisation, such co-operation is paramount. You may talk of competition with other departments, and may sometimes engage in forms of rivalry, but it would be suicidal for the organisation overall if you really did compete with your colleagues as aggressively as the internal politicians would have you do. Your own first question to your customers (from other parts of the organisation) should also be 'How can I help you?'

Activity 1.5

How competitive or co-operative are your relations with each of the other groups for which you provide services or – in particular – work alongside? If relationships are competitive, why? If they are co-operative, do you make the most of that co-operation?

➡ RELATIONSHIP MARKETING

Derived from a philosophy of co-operation, and perhaps as a reaction against the aggressive competition promoted earlier in the 1980s, relationship marketing stresses that you should build positive relationships with your customers. In part, at least, it represents a recogniton of what I said earlier, namely that you make your profit across a number of sales, or (if you are in the public sector) you improve your performance across a number of contacts, not just through the first one. Indeed, the first 'sale' is often made at a loss, as it demands an investment in building the initial relationship – in getting to know your client and his or her 'business'. This investment traditionally used to be thrown away as salesmen started afresh, to contact their next (new) 'cold' prospect! In fact, the whole strange culture of sales used to revolve around making just those one-off sales. The fabled difficulties involved were legendary in sales circles – and, of course, sales campaigns really were difficult where there was no existing relationship and no trust. If, however, you choose to build on that first contact, you can make later 'sales' without anywhere as near as much invest-ment of your time – and, indeed, you find that (with greater trust on both sides) your performance gets better with every new (repeat) sale.

Sheep and goats

This does, however, imply that you are making a real investment in the new customer. So you will need to be convinced that this investment will pay off over time; over a number of sales. The first rule of relationship marketing, therefore, is that you should make absolutely certain that you are marketing to people who need and want your product or service. If they don't, they simply won't come back for a second helping and you will almost inevitably lose money on the deal! In the old days, the measure of a good salesman was how well he was able to overcome the objections of the prospect; to sell him something he didn't want. That is the very reverse of relationship marketing. As I said earlier, making such a sale is very unproductive. Not only will it take even more time and effort than any other first sale, where there are usually plenty more customers to be recruited elsewhere, but it will not result in a follow-on sale because the customer will soon realise he has been conned. Worse still, it will ruin your reputation with that customer and with his or her many friends and acquaintances.

Surprisingly, therefore, the first rule of marketing – in any form – is to select those prospects who really are likely to buy. And the real measure of a good salesperson is how well he or she rejects as a waste of time those prospects who are not likely to buy. Indeed, the acid test of sales personnel's time management is how well they say *no* to time-wasters!

This, of course, would be true even if you were making just the one sale. Where you are planning to make repeat sales, then your attitude must be very different; you must almost welcome the customer into your extended family! So, the first task is always to find out what the prospect really wants; so you can judge whether you can provide that and, beyond that, enter into a productive long-term relationship. And that last point is not just a throwaway: even if you can easily make the first sale, you may not be able to build on it for later sales, and so you have to ask whether it is a sound investment of your time. The essence of good relationship marketing is how the relationship develops *over time*, over the longer term. And the core of this is the development of trust, so that both sides implicitly trust each other.

Activity 1.6

What is your organisation's relationship with its customers? Might it be regarded as a genuine 'relationship', even if it isn't called that? If not, why not? Do you trust your customers, and do they trust you?

Investment over time

This brings us to an aspect of relationship marketing that is only now starting to emerge, and is still unrecognised by most organisations: the relationship over time and, in particular, the investment in the relationship that that implies. Traditionally, marketing has been seen as a current cost. The implication has almost been that you should begrudge anything spent on promotion – perhaps as a necessary evil, but certainly only as a short-term cost. Indeed, a number of organisations facing harder times in the 1980s actually cut promotional spending, as you would expect them to do if they simply saw it as an unwelcome cost. Symbolically, promotional expenditure is generally recorded in a company's account as a cost on the profits and loss statement rather than on the balance sheet – but it should be in the latter if the investment aspect is to be taken into account.

In fact, most forms of promotion – in particular, advertising in the consumer goods field and relationship management in selling – take time to have an effect. Thus, spending money now on 'image' advertising may not reap maximum results for a year or more; and, equally, dropping expenditure now may not cause an obvious loss of momentum for a number of months. The pitfall that a number of organisations (not least IBM) fell into in the 1980s was thinking that, as a result of these 'cost savings' (without any immediate loss of sales momentum), they had found a new level of marketing efficiency! Indeed, the impact of promotion in general is not just long-term but *cumulative*. Regardless of what the bean-counters think, it should be clearly seen as an investment process; and we will look at this aspect later in the book. It should be considered in much the same context as other investment items, such as capital equipment, on the balance sheet. In particular, the investment in brand position or customer relationship must be safeguarded in the same way as any other corporate investment. You do not see plant managers stopping all maintenance on the production lines, because this will cut costs!

The only significant exception to all of this is the money spent on sales promotions – most typically price promotions: money off! This really does have a short-term impact, and is a true running cost in that all the evidence suggests that money spent in this way may improve sales in the short-term (as short-sighted marketers want) but at an uneconomic cost. It is paradoxical, therefore, that the greatest increase in promotion during the 1980s was on such sales promotion, so that it now accounts for more than half the total marketing budget, in an unproductive waste of investment potential.

Activity 1.7

Does your organisation view marketing expenditure as an investment or as a cost? How, then, does it expect to protect its position with (its investment in) the customer?

How do you see your group's relationship with its customers? Do they waste your time, or do you enjoy meeting them?

➡ THE FUNCTION OF MARKETING

Now let us look at the other end of the spectrum, at the functional elements of marketing. In most organisations these are typically encapsulated in a sales or marketing department that is formally responsible for contact – in person or via the media – with the customer. Within this function, a whole range of specialist techniques are deployed; and it is often these that are seen, by the general public, as 'marketing'.

These can be split most obviously between market research (finding out what the customers want) at one extreme and advertising (telling them what you have actually got) at the other – though, in the case of selling, the two can look much the same. Unfortunately, much of the functional aspect has been bogged down in the sort of obscure language that aspiring professionals often use to keep outsiders at bay. Indeed, we are now saddled with a 'profession' of marketing, with its insiders, which is silly when you consider that the whole aim of marketing should be to bring the outside world into the organisation! My intention, in this context, is to try to simplify some of these unnecessary complications, to demystify them.

The marketing dialogue

The best way to appreciate what is happening is to think of it as a dialogue. In the case of face-to-face selling, that is exactly what is happening, with the 'conversation' taking place between the sales person and the customer. Here, the dialogue starts with the salesperson asking a lot of questions in order to establish what the customer wants. It is reckoned that the best sales professionals listen for more than two-thirds of the time: they are good listeners, rather than having the gift of the gab as most people would expect! As we will see later, in Chapter 5 on selling, in practice this is not as easy as it might seem; but at this stage it offers a very useful picture of what is going on.

Only when the sales person fully understands what the customer wants should he or she switch into the other mode of explaining to the customer what is available to match these wants; switching from asking to telling, from listening to talking. Exactly the same basic process should happen across all forms of marketing. Thus, in the consumer goods markets you use market research to find out what groups of customers want and advertising is deployed to tell them what you have to match that. In database marketing, the customer's file – derived from purchases under a club membership say – will tell you what they probably will want next, and some form of direct 'mail' will then be used to tell them exactly what you have to match that. The emphasis here is on 'exactly', since you can now deal in this way with the individual rather than the group.

In essence, the most powerful form of marketing must be face-to-face selling, so long as this is conducted by good salespeople – of which there are, unfortunately, still too few. Suppliers of mass consumer goods only use advertising (for instance) because they cannot afford to fund the many millions of face-to-face contacts that would be necessary to sell baked beans in that way. So they seek out the statistics that tell them what groups want and then, by their seductive commercials, they try to convince members of these groups – you and me, perhaps – that we have experienced something similar to a face-to-face contact, and they hope that this is as persuasive.

But it can never be so, for the essence of effective marketing is interaction, and especially listening. Indeed, to put it brutally, you are wasting your breath until you know exactly what the customer wants and how you can meet that want; only then should you speak. That is the idea the book will follow, with the next few chapters talking about the customers and how you can find out about them through the various forms of formal and informal market research. To match the customer's wants, you should then examine the product or service you have on offer (and we shall do the same in this book), possibly with some surprising results. Only in the second half of the book will we look at how you can talk to your customers with the aim of explaining how well you can match their needs and wants.

Within the overall split between listening and talking (and especially the latter), there are a number of sub-topics that greatly fascinate practitioners and academics such as myself – and some of these may even be important in specific cases! These are often referred to as 'the marketing mix'. Accordingly, we will investigate a number of these sub-topics in later chapters. In the process I will try to demystify some of the myths of advertising and of public relations, which are much more a matter of common sense than of glamour. And I will look at the problem of price – which stampedes too many managers into frenzies of price-cutting – and of the soothing effects of sound strategic planning; and, in particular, of long-range marketing, which too few organisations consider.

➡ SELLING TO YOUR STAKEHOLDERS

Especially, though, we will look at the magic of selling, to see if some of it can rub off on you. For, although I have talked so far about customers, there are actually a range of participants in the processes of marketing. These are, rather formally, described as 'stakeholders' (or even worse as 'publics'!). But all this term means is the people who have an interest in any sales achieved, and there are more of these people than you might expect.

Thus, at the customer end there are others involved. Not least are the consumers, the family for whom the baked beans are bought and who have a very direct influence on the choice; and the members of their peer group, your existing customers, who recommend the product in the first place. At your (supplier's) end, there are all your workers involved in offering the product, and especially the service, whom you have to persuade – by inner marketing (of which more later) – to do their very best for the customers; and your own suppliers; and the local community, which claims to have an interest; and so on and so on. It is surprising just how many people you need to convince, all of whom are susceptible, in one way or another, to the charms of marketing.

Activity 1.8

Who are your organisation's key stakeholders; customers; employees, suppliers, local communities, etc?

Who are your own group's stakeholders? What does each of these groups of stakeholders want from you and your group?

Chapter 2
The customer as hero

We now move on to investigate the 'hero' of this book, the customer. As we have seen, in organisations that genuinely have adopted a marketing philosophy everything starts with the customer, and all the subsequent processes are, in one way or another, focused on that customer. So, marketers need to know as much as possible about their customers. Indeed, since we all have customers for our work – the other departments that take our services within the organisation, say – we *all* need to understand our customers.

➡ PIGEON-HOLING CONSUMERS

Traditionally, this understanding has been achieved by sorting these customers into a series of pigeon-holes. In the consumer goods field, where this form of categorisation has reached its peak of perfection, they have traditionally been grouped in terms of age, gender and social class. All of these groupings seem to make sense; it is not unreasonable to expect tht a middle-aged upper-class woman will have rather different tastes and (more important from the marketer's point of view) buying habits from those of a teenage working-class male. For many years now, this form of classification has been the simple basis for consumer goods marketing. In particular, it has been the approach offered by the owners of television stations, newspapers and magazines as the basis for justifying their presence in the media package that is supposed to offer the best coverage of the 'target audience' (the people who you think are most likely to take your product or service).

More recently, the effectiveness of this categorisation has been questioned, not least by some of the researchers with whom I work. Even so, let us start with these categories, because they are simple to understand as well as simple to use.

Age

The first category is very easy to determine. Almost everyone, anywhere in the world, now knows how old they are, and they are happy to allocate themselves to an age category. Most important of all, perhaps, the media track this as a prime factor in what they offer to advertisers. And age does matter. As we have seen, teenagers buy rather different things from the middle-aged; and the latter in turn have needs different from pensioners. If you want older people, you will select certain types of magazines; if you want teenagers, you may choose cinema advertising.

More recently, though, the leading-edge marketers have chosen to use *lifestages* rather than age alone, although they do run parallel to each other. Lifestages also take account or the major events that change buying behaviour. Single people get married; they then, in general, have babies, which can have the greatest impact of all and in a matter of a few months transform the new parents' way of life. Then they spend many years bringing up their family, as young children grow into teenagers and eventually leave home. This leaves the couple alone once more ('empty-nesters', in lifestage jargon), with relatively high incomes and only themselves to spend it on. Each of these stages results in quite different buying behaviours, and quite different opportunities for astute marketers! However, it is worth noting that most organisations – most notably in the media industry – still use age rather than lifestage as the guide to their marketing activities.

Activity 2.1

How have your own buying habits changed over the years, as you have got older? How have they changed as you have reached the various 'lifestage' watersheds?

Gender

This category is, again, easy to determine. But it has become very controversial; hence my careful use of the word gender (which is socially determined) rather than sex (which is biologically determined). Even so, there are very clear differences in behaviour and, though it is politically incorrect now to talk about it, the ubiquitous housewife is still the main buyer for the family, although she may now be in full-time employment like her male partner.

It used to be much clearer cut. The woman as housewife was the only target for consumer goods companies; she bought everything for the family, apart from 'masculine' things like cars. Now all that has changed. Women aspire to very different things (there are even car advertisements aimed at women), and they are as likely to be breadwinners as their men-folk; so that, not least, they have much less time to identify with the old stereotype of the housewife who spent much of each week cleaning, baking and shopping for essentials. Even so, and here I may offend the feminists, gender still proves to be a very useful categorisation in many markets. And, of course, it is one that many suppliers still use, especially in the fashion industry.

Social class

This grouping used to be a mainstay of market categorisation, and still is the mainstay used by much of the media; the broadsheets are proud to be 'up-market' with, literally, a higher class of readers. But there has been considerable debate recently about how relevant this form of classification is. It is claimed that the boundaries are blurring, and in particular we are all becoming middle-class. This is an exaggeration, for in the UK nearly one-third are still working class (category D or E, according to the scales used by advertising agencies), and one-sixth are upper class (A or B), but rather more than half are now middle-class (so much so that the classification has had to be split into C1 and C2). Although the advantage of classification is that it allows you to split the population into separate groups that are easier to process and profile, the fact that the middle class now covers so many people undermines the approach.

In addition, class is quite difficult to determine. It is – as used by advertising agencies, at least – an awkward mixture of income level (highly relevant as it shows how much you have to spend) and social status (which may suggest how you might spend it). In terms of its use in practice, it requires a subjective decision by an interviewer on social position (which may come from occupation or inheritance), and research shows that interviewers can be wrong in up to 20% of cases. Nevertheless, interviewers' mistakes seem to cancel out, and research has shown that social class is still a reasonable indicator of purchasing behaviour; so you should not write off class just yet. It remains one of the most powerful and – despite the difficulties – practical ways of separating out groups with different patterns of behaviour.

Activity 2.2

What class are you? What class are your friends? Does this influence your, or their, buying habits?

Lifestyle

The major new dimension, which has emerged over recent decades, is that of lifestyle. This was initially driven by an approach called VALS (Value Added LifeStyles), developed by SRI International, which looked at how people chose to live their lives in different ways – different from the way the old categorisations would have predicted. It separated people into new categories, such as those who are 'outer-directed' (in other words influenced by the world outside themselves) and those who are 'inner-directed'. A whole range of sub-categories was also constructed, such as 'achievers', 'belongers', 'survivors' and the 'societally conscious', who were each supposed to behave in very different ways.

This approach, and others like it that were developed, became very fashionable – not least with advertising agencies, who liked the freedom it gave to their creative work. It has now even extended to the social sciences, which have used it to bolster their ideas as to what 'post-modernism' means. It can, indeed, be a powerful device for looking at some groups of customers, especially in fashion markets; but research indicates that, even so, it is still not as powerful a differentiator of behaviour as social class. Nevertheless, at the end of the day, *any* way that can help you focus on specific customer behaviours is helpful.

Activity 2.3

How would you describe your lifestyle(s)? Is it significantly different from what you perceive for the rest of the population? How? Why? Is it significantly different from what might have been assumed on the basis of your class? How has it changed over recent years?

➡ OTHER PIGEON-HOLES FOR CONSUMERS

There are other ways of categorising individuals. Geography can be quite important in some cases. For instance, in the United States there are significant differences between purchasing patterns in New England (Boston) and the South-West (Dallas), if for no other reason than the weather! And then there are ethnic groups. In California, the Hispanics have their own television stations, so they needn't even speak English, let alone buy the same products as their white Anglo-Saxon neighbours!

Then there is a whole range of psychological factors that people have proposed. The most famous is probably the 'hierarchy of needs' proposed by Abraham Maslow. This starts at the bottom with physiological needs (literally those needed to survive) and runs up to esteem (the conspicuous consumption that some 'achievers' indulge in so as to impress their neighbours) and then to self-actualisation (the inner-directed self-fulfilment that the societally-conscious aim for). As there is little to distinguish between these two upper levels, I tended to ignore this approach – until I taught in Ethiopia, where I found that the lower levels were definitely significant because 'physiological needs' really means something for people who are starving!

➡ **ORGANISATIONAL PURCHASING**

So far we have looked at how consumer goods companies see their individual customers – people like you and me. Now we will briefly look at the equivalent positions in the industrial goods and services markets, where we are selling to organisations rather than to individuals. In some of these markets, the position may not be too different: if, for example, we are selling consumables to large numbers of small purchasers – copier paper to individual departments, or light bulbs to building services – the end result might look much the same.

On the other hand, a significant part of these markets does operate very differently; in a way that is best described as leading to a 'complex' sale. In the first instance, it may be more complex because the product or service is inherently more complex: the purchase of a complete new assembly line requires more thought than that of a can of baked beans. Then it may be more complex in terms of the extended timescales: where you might buy the beans as an impulse purchase on the spur of the moment, the assembly line purchasing process will certainly extend over a number of months, and possibly over years. Finally, it may be complex because there are a number of people involved in the buying decision: you may make your own decision on the beans, but the assembly line decision will involve a number of factory managers and engineers, people from development, from finance and administration, and – most important of all – the senior management budget-holders. Decisions of that size will probably involve all members of the board, but they may include people from across the organisation, even including marketers (as a brand manager I even once bought an assembly line myself – over the heads of the production people!)

Accordingly, you can't view such industrial purchasing decisions as simple, with just one meeting between a buyer and a salesperson (as much of sales training assumes), and they fully justify the description 'complex'. They will typically involve a number of such meetings with a range of people. Some academics have tried to define the various groups involved. The common factor that most of these frameworks seem to share is splitting people into groups who are 'decision makers' (the budget holders, say, who have the authority to take the decision to buy) or 'influencers' (who have the right to sway which way the decision will go). Some add a further category, which is 'gatekeepers': those who – usually for technical reasons (including purchasing rules) – can veto the decision.

These distinctions are useful. Recognition that the ultimate decision maker is the budget holder, usually a board member, is a salutary reminder to the salesperson who has spent several months calling on a junior buyer that he or she has a lot more work to do before making a sale! In fact, most sales personnel *never* obtain access to the key decision makers! But real life is even more complex than these splits would allow for. The most obvious example of this is the fact that the 'influencers' normally include the 'users' – and, in most organisations, their views carry as much weight as those of formally appointed decision makers. After all, the users are the people who will have to make the decision work in practice. In effect, in most situations they – whatever the rule-book says – are the de facto decision makers, but many sales personel don't even call on these key 'customers'!

The importance of recognising all these participants in the selling process is to remind the marketers (the sales personnel) that they must understand the role of each of them in the process. There is an easy solution, which few marketers follow through, and that is simply to cover *all* the bases, to talk to *all* of these people – or as many as possible. If in doubt, in marketing, always get the customer's view! In my experience, most sales campaigns fail because the sales personnel haven't even talked to the real decision maker, because the real buyers are rarely to be found in the comfortable surroundings of the purchasing department!

Activity 2.4

In your own group, who are the overall decision makers, and who are the key ones in the context of decisions on suppliers? Do your suppliers recognise this fact?

Who are the decision makers and influencers amongst your own (internal) customers? How do you take this into account in your dealings with them?

Who do you think are the key decision makers and influencers amongst your organisation's customers? Do you have any contact with them?

➡ CONSUMERS AND END USERS

As I have already hinted, there are layers of influence in all purchasing, including that in consumer markets. The most obvious of these are the consumer of consumer goods and the end user of industrial goods. These are the people who may never be directly involved in the buying decision, but whose views represent a crucial indirect element. The mother buys the baby food, and she knows which ones the baby spits out. The vending machine supplies buyer will not order drinks that the staff hate. So, marketers need to take into account the needs and wants of these consumers just as much as those of the direct customers. IBM's failure to do so in the PC market ultimately led to its downfall.

➡ MEASURING SALES

Volume of usage

But even the purchasers themselves buy very different amounts of the product or service. So, one of the most important characteristics of consumers and customers is the amount they buy. Consumer goods companies talk about 'heavy' users versus 'light' users, and industrial marketers about 'large' ('key') accounts versus 'small'. The reason for this split is simple. The heavy users are worth more, typically *much* more, to the organisation than the small ones; so they are more important, and suppliers should put more effort into the recruiting and holding such accounts. The two are, in industrial markets, typically treated in very different ways. The large accounts will be personally serviced by a team, often headed up by a manager (the account manager), whereas the small ones will be subcontracted to outside agents, dealers or wholesalers.

This fact is recognised by what is probably the most important 'rule' in the whole of marketing theory; the 80:20 Rule. We will return to this idea a number of times throughout the book, but in the context of this section it quite simply says that 80% of your business will come from 20% of your customers; and these are the ones you must most carefully guard.

Who are the 20% of your organisation's most important customers? Does the organisation single them out for special treatment? If so, what? If not, why not?

How about your own group's 20% of key internal customers? Do they account for the largest part of your activity? How do you treat them?

Product (brand) shares

Sales levels are, of course, important. But they may not tell the whole story. Your sales may be going up, but those of others in the market may be growing even faster; so your share is falling. When a boom, say, comes to an end, you may find your overall position has weakened.

Perhaps the most important measure of performance is, therefore, that of the share of the overall business in the market. This is often referred to as 'brand share', and we will look at brands (as opposed to raw products) later. At first sight, this can be a confusing topic because there can be a number of such measures, all of which look very similar. First of these may be *penetration*, which is easy to measure but simply shows the (percentage) number of potential customers who use a product or service. But even this may be confusing, for – as we have seen above – they might be heavy or light users; unlike voters, not all customers are equal.

So more important is *product share*, the share of the overall market volume being purchased by these customers, the share of the overall total business taken by your organisation. Even the share of volume does not, however, tell all. One brand may be more expensive – the brand leader can usually justify a price premium over the other runners – so that the *value* of its share may be higher than the volume would indicate. Accordingly, most marketers consider that the most important measure of brand share is to be seen in terms of value. It is, though, more difficult to measure. Clearly you should know the value of your own sales, although what they fetch in a supermarket rather than at list prices is not always obvious. But to know the figure for the overall market, and for your competitors, you have to find some way of recording everything customers across the market buy. In consumer goods markets, you will usually take this data from market research companies; in industrial markets, all you may have are government figures of sometimes dubious quality (at one time, sales of typewriters were reported by the UK government in terms of total weight!).

Activity 2.6

What share(s) of its market(s) does your organisation have? This may be a difficult question to answer (even for your senior management), so try a simpler one: is it a market leader or a small niche player?

Gap analysis

What the bare figures do not show is *why* differences exist. This is the subject of 'gap analysis', which at its basic level recognises that there is a gap between what you are achieving and what you (or your shareholders) might want to achieve. This can have a number of components. At the top level, and ignored by most suppliers, there is a *usage gap*, between the level of sales actually being achieved across all brands in the market – market sales – and the potential level that might be achieved if all the customers bought as much as they might ultimately want. The problem here is that, as we have seen, even the actual sales levels are difficult to measure, and potential sales can only be guessed at on the basis of market research.

Below this, we arrive at some more meaningful gaps. The *distribution gap* for a product reflects the shortfall in its distribution, which means that not all potential customers even get access to it to buy it. This may be because the supermarkets will not stock it, or that it is limited to one geographical area. In an industrial market, you may be limiting yourself to certain types of customer (makers of military aircraft but not airliners, say). The solution is to improve that distribution – though, if the supermarkets will only stock the brand leaders and you aren't one, tough luck!

The next gap is the *product gap*, which represents how well your product or service measures up to the needs of the overall market. It may be limited – by design (as we will see later in this chapter) or by default – to certain groups of customers. Excluded groups will not even consider buying it.

The final gap is the *competitive gap*. This represents how effectively you market your offering (the same product to the same customers) as compared with your competitors. It is probably what you thought marketing was all about but, as we have seen, it is usually only a small part of the overall picture.

Every marketer worth his or her salt struggles to maximise potential, distribution, product match and competitiveness!

Activity 2.7

Look at your organisation's activities and see how it might close the gaps it faces.

Try the same for the work of your own group. Are there fresh things you could do to narrow some of the gaps? Are your services available to the widest possible range of internal users? If you added to, or changed, your services, would more of these internal users be helped?

➡ PURCHASE BEHAVIOUR

Diffusion of product usage

One aspect of purchase behaviour that is often ignored by otherwise sophisticated marketers is the extent to which it is influenced by others, and in particular by other members of the purchaser's peer group (the people they see to be like themselves, whose views and advice they respect). Thus, research indicates that the buying decision is not as simple as advertisers would like to think. Customers do not just see an advert and immediately rush out and buy the product; in fact, it seems likely that they are often more influenced by what their peers say. So the process is an indirect one: the peers see the advert, try the product and then recommend it to their friends.

Nevertheless, some groups of buyers are much more adventurous than others. They are the first people, for instance, to try a new product; and they relate their experience to others, who also try it – and then, over time, more and more people are recruited to the brand. In academic circles, the very first group of users, just a couple of per cent perhaps, is referred to as the 'innovators'. Then the 'early adopters' follow them, and eventually the mass of the population comes too; with the 'laggards' bringing up the rear. The point of this observation is that there can be a number of different processes at work at the same time. Indeed, in launching a new product, you will probably have to invest a great deal of effort in recruiting the very small group of initial users (the innovators), but the investment will hopefully be justified when these act as the advance guard of the army that they go out and recruit.

So the curve of new product sales starts gently but then accelerates as the early adopters arrive, and only plateaus when the laggards are reached. In the case of most products, it can take months or even years (research indicates it may be up to a decade) to really establish a new product. This may not always be the case, however: where there is a fashion (or fad) involved, the sales can rise almost immediately – but beware, for they are then likely to fall almost as fast!

Activity 2.8

Who are the 'innovators' and 'early adopters' for your organisation's products or services? And who are the 'laggards'?

Who represent those categories in terms of your own group's work? How do you take account of this?

Loyalty

Once you have established a mature product in a stable market, then another measure which is often used is loyalty. You are endeavouring to establish a customer base of loyal users, people who will buy your product or service in preference to your competitors, time and time again. This clearly offers a major marketing advantage, and some significant marketing theory is built around this. In practice, as my fellow researchers have observed, it is – yet again – more complex than at first appears. Customers, in some markets at least, do not just buy the same brand week after week; instead, they tend to buy portfolios of brands (where they often get bored with the same brand each time). In this context, 'loyalty' is simply redefined as a greater likelihood of choosing your brand as against others, and the end result is much the same.

In industrial markets, where portfolio buying seems less prevalent, loyalty is even more important. It is sometimes assumed that when an industrial organisation wants to buy more of a product, it will go through the whole purchase process. This is true the first time a purchase is made – a new buy – but thereafter nothing could be further from the truth. The purchasing process is almost as painful for the buyers as for the sales personnel; so it is a last resort, only if all else fails do you repeat the whole process. Normally, if everything seems to be going well and the suppliers have not blotted their copybooks, a repeat purchase – a rebuy – is made almost automatically. It is usually only if the supplier has failed in some way that others are invited to tender for the business – a modified rebuy.

This has some important implications. Not least is that maintaining your existing customers, meeting their every need and want with a consistently high level of service, has to be your highest priority. You should never allow the least excuse for a customer to go out to competitive tender. Opening that door may prove to be very expensive. At the other extreme, if you want to become a supplier, you have to judge very carefully the situations that seem to be open to you – too many of the buyers may be merely going through the motions – so that you can focus on the *real* business, the sales that are achievable.

Activity 2.9

How loyal are your organisation's customers? How does it reward this loyalty? How loyal are your own group's customers?

Models of purchase behaviour

Marketing textbooks, my own included, are replete with all sorts of models of buyer behaviour; indeed some academics seem to think of nothing else! The reality is that, whilst they might sometimes help you understand buyer behaviour, they are rarely able to predict it. It is much easier, as we shall see in the next chapter, simply to go out and conduct some suitable market research. I make no excuse for repeating the maxim, 'If you don't know the answer, ask the customer'.

A very simple model of the purchase process, though, can help you understand some of the stages the buyer may go through before buying a product or service. I suppose the most often quoted one, not least by sales trainers, is AIDA (Attention, Interest, Desire, Action). Perhaps a more realistic model, albeit without a memorable acronym, is one that has rather better defined stages: Awareness, Interest, Understanding, Attitude and Buying Decision.

The first stage of *awareness* should be self-evident, since if the potential purchaser is not even aware of the need for your product or service, there is no way that they will buy it! But beyond that, and this model is usually applied to advertising, the first need is to create *interest* in what the product or service can do for the potential customer before they will even consider it. And then, the next stage is *understanding* what the product or service is and why a customer should want to buy it. The stage after that is where they should start to develop positive *attitudes* towards it, and that in turn should lead on to the *buying decision*.

This is a very simple model, but as such it applies quite generally to industrial markets as well as consumer ones. But it misses one major point, which we have explored in these first two chapters, and that is that most purchase decisions revolve around repeat purchases. It is the history, developed over the longer term, that really counts, and it is certainly the progression of such sales that builds organisational performance levels. So we like to take the process further, beyond that first purchase.

Once the product or service has been tried, hopefully with more than satisfactory results, you then enter into the repeat purchase process, which follows a rather different set of rules. Not least of these is the one that says your first priority is maintaining the customer's loyalty, almost regardless of cost. This imposes a contradictory set of conditions on many mass-marketing campaigns, which must be designed to recruit new users, according to one set of rules, and at the same time to maintaining existing users, according to another. It is no wonder that so few mass-marketing campaigns are really successful, especially where most marketers do not even recognise the dilemma and treat everyone as if they are first-time buyers! The sales people who can concentrate on the specific needs of each prospect or customer have a much easier time.

But it is important to recognise the difference in the sales process that exist between first and subsequent purchases. Before the first purchase, you need to persuade the prospect to try the product. After that, you want to retain them with an ongoing positive experience. Coca-Cola famously fell into the trap when it abandoned the old product, because PepsiCo was recruiting more new users, and replaced it with a sweeter product that tasted, at first, more interesting. When it launched its new formulation, however, it found that it was alienating its existing customers (who quickly became bored with the sickly-sweet formulation), and Coca-Cola's management had a desperate recovery exercise on its hands – one which, to give due credit, it completed successfully.

In fact, the two sets of rules need not be as far apart as they might seem, for the 'diffusion' behaviour we looked at earlier in this chapter means that most new purchasers do not come to a supplier directly but are brought in indirectly by existing users. So, contrary to what most marketing textbooks would have you believe, you should – once you have recruited the 'innovators' and 'early adopters' – focus above all on retaining your loyal customers, who will in turn bring in the new customers.

My own model, which takes these wider elements into account, is shown in Figure 2.1. This embodies most of the essentials of the wider process. Thus, the central pillar (the consumer's progress) highlights the tentative nature of the first stages as the consumer moves from 'susceptibility' to the actual purchase, and then the no less important subsequent stages as confidence builds into loyalty.

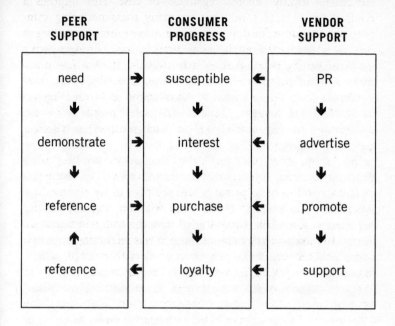

Figure 2.1: The three pillars of the purchasing process

The break point, at the time of the first (trial) purchase, is reflected in the vendor's pillar by the switch from 'promotion' to 'support' (though this aspect is rarely emphasised in theory). It is even more obvious in the peer support pillar in the switch from 'taker' (of advice, or 'reference') before first purchase to 'giver' (as a loyal referee) after purchase.

Activity 2.10

Who does your organisation aim its promotional or sales activities at: existing or new customers? How does it maintain existing customers? How effective is it in doing this? What changes would you suggest?

➡ MARKETS

So far, in this chapter, I have been talking about individual customers. But there are very few organisations that can survive on the business of just one customer. Instead you need a number of customers and, together with the customers loyal to your competitors, these build up into what is called 'the market'. Once again, the definition is, though, more complex than it may at first seem. It starts with the customers, but more practically it is based on the business coming from all of these. Such a market may be geographically based (the North American market, say), for after all the very word 'market' in this context derives from the town market where the local peasants sold their goods. As favoured by suppliers, it may be based alternatively on the products or services being offered (the baked beans or banking markets, for instance), or on the industries they are sold to (the health services market – which could, of course, include sales of baked beans to hospitals), or on the psychological measures they consider important (such as the luxury goods market – which is unlikely to include baked beans!)

For marketers, though, the best definition must be in terms of the customers buying in a certain market, either as individuals with recognisably similar requirements or as the business they generate. Of course, this often turns out to be the same as that defined by the 'products', but the shifted focus is, as always in marketing, important. It also means that wider potential can be explored; the entertainment market is much wider than that for feature films – which is why the Disney Corporation got into running theme parks.

Activity 2.11

What market(s) is your organisation in? Which ones(s) is your group in?

Market segments

Within each main market, though, there may be a number of sub-

markets that share many common features within the overall
market, as all cars do, but with some which distinguish them from
other sub-markets (as luxury cars differ, for instance, from ordinary
saloons in the car market). At this point there can be problems
with terminology; some academics tend to refer to these sub-
markets as 'segments' of the main market, as I will do, but some
reserve this term for only those parts differentiated by intangible
factors (such as emotional feel). Whichever definition is adopted,
segmentation is a very powerful marketing device. As we shall see
later, there are many benefits coming from being a brand leader,
and the minor brands are put at a disadvantage. There can be only
one *market* leader, but many benefits are also available to the
segment leaders, and there can be more of these.

So there are considerable benefits for some suppliers in focusing
on individual segments. These are parts of the markets where
groups of customers share similar requirement characteristics (the
diet versions of baked beans, say, or the rigorous quality demanded
of bolts for the aviation industry). The important aspect is that
these characteristics allow you to group customers together into a
segment which you can sell to. They must be sufficiently different
from other segments that you can separate them out, but
sufficiently similar to each other that you can focus on them; and
there must be enough of them to make their business worthwhile.
At the extreme, usually in retail markets, a 'niche market' is so
small a segment that it can only support one supplier – which
keeps all the others out (unless the market leader decides it is
worthwhile paying some attention, as happened to Sock Shop in
the UK, when Marks & Spencer virtually destroyed it!)

So the first question for you is 'What market am I in?' But the
second, and often the more important, one is 'What segments are
there, and which of these can I profitably exploit by focusing my
efforts on them so that I can effectively become the segment
leader?' This technique is usually exploited by larger organisations,
but paradoxically it may be especially important for smaller
companies because it offers them their only opportunity to gain
the benefits of segment domination!

Activity 2.12

Is the market in which your organisation operates segmented? If
so, what account does it take of these segments, and which does it
target? Which should it target?

Positioning

So, you've decided on a segment you want to target. How do you
achieve that targeting? The answer is that you position your brand
to do exactly that. You need to make the brand meet the specific
needs of the segment or, more likely, you need to tell the
customers in that segment how it meets their wants.

This is classically represented as a 'positioning map', one such
being shown in Figure 2.2. This is a means of visualising what you
need to do. In the very simplified picture of Figure 2.2, the
customers in segment 1 want reasonably high quality and are

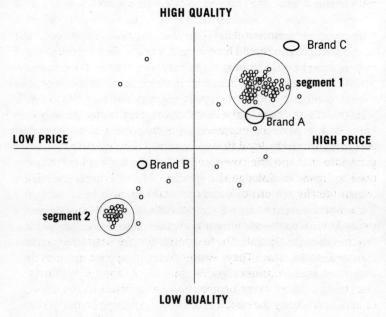

Figure 2.2: A positioning map

willing to pay a reasonably high price for this. Thus, Brand A could reposition itself, by raising quality, so that it sits nicely in the centre of this segment and very effectively target it. Brand C, though, can reduce its quality a lot (and price a bit) to achieve much the same result! In both cases, the map is a way of visualising what needs to be done.

Beware, however, because the dimensions are not necessarily the ones you – as a supplier – imagine are important. They must be the ones that are important to the customers in that segment!

Activity 2.13

As a very crude approximation, try to draw a positioning map of the various segments – along with the positions of your own organisation's brands and its competitors – in terms of the two main 'dimensions' that you think are important to your customers.

➡ THE CUSTOMER FRANCHISE AND BRANDING

If you have been successful in doing all the things I have suggested in this chapter, you should have loyal customers who are dedicated to your brand. You can put a notional value on this loyalty, and this is the 'customer franchise'. It represents your investment in the customer and – what is often forgotten – their investment in your brand. It represents the outcome of all the many things you have done, and all the experiences the customer has had, which persuade them to be loyal to you. In view of all the effort that has gone into it – and the comparable effort that a competitor will need to invest to dislodge this loyalty – it can be very valuable (worth literally billions of dollars for some brands).

The *alter ego* of this customer franchise is the brand (investment) value. Thus, after mentioning it a number of times, at long last I can introduce 'the brand'. The first point to make is that people get confused about this. They assume it only applies to heavily advertised mass-consumer goods. In fact, it applies to almost everything. Almost every organisation has a brand of some sort, even if, as is usually the case, it is the company name or, in the case of the government sector, a department name – indeed, in recent history some such departments have been the most avid users of branding! In terms of how you handle your brands, there are a number of possible policies:

- **company name**: as we have seen (especially in the industrial sector), it is often just the company's name that is promoted;
- **family branding**: in this case, a very strong branding name (or company name) is made the vehicle for a range of products; and
- **individual branding** is where each brand has a separate name and may even compete against other brands from the same company.

In terms of existing products, brands may be developed in a number of ways:

- **brand extension**: an existing strong brand name can be used as a vehicle for new or modified products, and this appears to be the most prevalent form of development nowadays, which is understandable since it maximises the use of the investment in the brand name.
- **multibrands**: alternatively, in a market that is fragmented amongst a number of brands, a supplier can choose deliberately to launch totally new brands in apparent competition with its own existing strong brand(s).

The important point to note is that, even if you think you do not have a brand, your customers will apply one to you in one form or another; and you had better protect this investment.

We all recognise the Coca-Cola brand, but my own organisation's name – The Open University – is one of the most powerful brands in the UK. It simply arose because it describes what we are (in much the same way that International Business Machines, IBM, did), but in the minds of the public it now goes way beyond that. In the first instance, it is highly recognisable – most people in the UK will spontaneously quote it (or its equally well known diminutive, the OU) when asked for the name of a university. But it is also powerful (as a brand should be) and, beyond that, exudes 'warm' values – excellence, equality and everything you might ever want. It is this wonderful *image* that makes the OU brand even more powerful.

Thus, the brand is a peg on which you can hang all the positive things, especially the intangibles, that you want to say about your product or services or organisation. It encompasses the actual physical products, plus the ephemeral services, together with all that you say about it and yourself. It creates the psychological factors and the attitudes that persuade customers to place their business with you. Indeed, the best way of thinking of a brand is as the *personality* of your product or service or organisation. In consumer goods, it is quite often recommended that you try to imagine your brand as a family friend. That is not bad advice, because the customer would like to feel as comfortable with the brands they commit to as with the friends they choose!

The power of branding comes on a number of fronts. It means that you can lock your customers into something that is not just a physical product (which might rapidly become outdated). The classical example is, once more, Coca-Cola. After all, it is just flavoured water – it long ago dropped the coca leaf ingredient that gave it its name. But, as PepsiCo has found over the years, it is not easy to displace this brand leader – no matter how much you spend on new formulations. Above all, though, it means that you can roll together all the things, especially the intangibles, that you want to associate with the brand, not least in your advertising.

In economic terms, the brand is even more powerfully a device to create a monopoly, or at least a form of imperfect competition, so that the brand owner can obtain some of the benefits that accrue to a monopoly, particularly those benefits related to decreased price competition.

The final outcome of this process, if you are lucky (and invest very large sums of money), is simply that you achieve the benefits offered by brand leadership, encapsulated in the 'Rule of 123'. This quite simply says that, in a mature and stable market (which most are), the brand leader can expect to hold twice the share of the second brand and three times the share of the third – and no other brand will make significant sales. You can see, therefore why brand leadership is so valuable. You gain all the benefits of scale in your production, and even so can actually sell at a higher price than anyone else; all of which means that the revenue streams give you a war chest sufficient to see off anyone who wants to displace your cash cow. The sheer power of the brand leader simply cannot be overestimated!

Activity 2.14

What is your organisation's brand(s)? Is it a specific name attached to its leading product(s) or service(s), or is it the company name? How does it use this brand name in its promotional activities? How does the brand leader in your market make use of its brand?

At a much lower level, what 'brand' might be applied to your own group? What do your internal customers call it (especially behind your back)?

Chapter 3
Listening to your customers

At the beginning of this book, I defined marketing in general as a dialogue: listening and then talking. Of these two activities, the one that encapsulates effective marketing is listening, the very reverse of what most people expect! You can't satisfy a customer's needs and wants until you have found out what these are; and that means you must listen to your customers very carefully indeed. Most textbooks describe this process as 'marketing research'. In common with most practitioners, I call it – albeit incorrectly – '*market* research', and throughout this book I will use the same terminology as those working in the field.

In any case, as I have already indicated, I think listening is a much more useful term, especially as it most often takes place in the form of face-to-face contact between suppliers and their customers – not just between sales personnel and buyers but amongst all those involved. So, mortally offending my fellow academics, I will start with how you find out about your customers when you talk to them face to face:

➡ QUESTIONING

The starting point for market research is the process of questioning customers and prospects. This might seem easy to achieve when you are asking questions based on your own personal interest, but most people are even then simply not very effective at asking such questions. They ask very specific (closed) questions which tend to narrow discussion; and, in particular, tend to confine the discussion to the areas set by their own personal preferences or prejudices. Much more useful are those (open) questions that allow the person being questioned to adopt a wider view. These questions (of which the simplest – Why? How? What? – are the most powerful) encourage the speaker to say what he or she considers is most important about the topic. The listener can then gain the most benefit from the speaker's knowledge and expertise. Later in the conversation, closed questions can be used to steer the conversation to the topics of greatest interest to the listener.

Open questions also seem to be the most difficult for a manager, perhaps such as you, to ask, possibly because they are not so obviously leading directly to the answer that is wanted. But they are the key to unlocking the tongue of the person facing you. If the conversation proceeds with very short replies (and particularly just 'yes' or 'no'), it is likely that you are not using enough open questions and may be missing the real issues. The more open the question, the better. The most powerful question is quite simply 'Why?', often closely followed by 'How?'

In practice, open questions come naturally if you are genuinely interested in finding out what makes the prospect's business tick. One successful, if little reported, way of getting round these problems is 'rambling', in other words giving the customer the time to ramble around the subject. This can be an enormous strain on the listener, for it is very difficult not to interrupt. But, in the same way as interrogation methods often depend upon allowing prisoners to ramble so that they inevitably give away too much of themselves, if the listener simply allows a speaker enough time – and does not interrupt his or her rambling – the full answers will emerge.

Even if managers do ask the correct open questions, they often undermine the progress by stopping the speaker in mid-flow. The natural accompaniment to an open question is silence. It is, though, a surprisingly aggressive technique, and you should not make it too obvious – it is best just to look very thoughtful. The person you are questioning will eventually feel obliged to talk, and usually what he or she then says is especially enlightening (since he or she too will have had time to consider).

As indicated above, closed questions, typically requiring the brief answer 'yes' or 'no', have (justifiably) received a bad press. But it is still necessary to use them quite extensively to clarify points. A problem only arises when such questions are used instead of open questions. In many situations, by far the most important closed questions (and arguably the most important questions of all) are those where you check for agreement. As the discussion progresses, it is imperative that you establish whether or not you are taking the other person with you (in case, as all too often happens, the person is in fact politely acting out the role of audience to your orator), and closed questions are very useful here.

But you must not just put good questions to a customer; you must listen to the answers. Many managers are too busy trying to put their own view across to hear what is being said in reply; and thus they miss much of the key information that is emerging. Listening implies far more than hearing. It also involves the process of analysing what is heard in order to understand it; to make sense of it in general, and then to put it into the intellectual framework of the organisational activities being discussed. Listening is a very active pursuit, not a passive one – or the listener will soon become a sleeper!

It is conventionally reckoned that a good questioner should spend two-thirds of the time listening and only one-third talking. What is important, though, is how you use that time. It is the quality of the listening (which has much to do with how you analyse what you hear) that is as important as the quantity.

Understanding

Thus, hearing, and even listening, is not enough. The key to questioning by managers is *understanding*. This is a process to which the main contribution must, of course, be made by what the person being questioned says, although it should be noted that this may include what he or she said in a number of previous meetings as well as in the current discussion. But it will also include all the other evidence that you have unearthed. Put it all together and, hopefully, you will be able to complete the jigsaw.

Understanding of informal communications is, therefore, a cumulative process that may span several discussions. It is an important skill for managers, yet it is often ignored by management educators.

So much for obtaining information from customers when you meet them. But, of course, market research goes beyond these informal contacts. A lot of the time you are not even talking face to face. Indeed, market research covers a great deal more and is, as I have said, the most important element of marketing. So we shall now look at the techniques that are used in the wider world of market research to see how you can obtain the best possible information on your customers and understand it.

Activity 3.1

After the next time you get involved in such a question-and-answer session, with one of your colleagues say, spend a few minutes thinking through, and preferably noting down, what happened in the meeting. Did you use enough open questions? Did you really understand what was being said?

At later meetings, try to listen more; and again review your performance afterwards.

➡ DESK RESEARCH

The starting point for market research in most cases will almost inevitably be the information that is already available. Quite often this can even be found in your *own* files – so these should be a good starting point. You may be surprised what you find there! When I worked for IBM, I once spent nearly £30,000 finding a supplier with the suitable leading-edge technology I needed; only to discover that they were another division of IBM!

The first thing you should do is select and organise those pieces of your own data that are relevant. In marketing, they are often most usefully organised into 'facts' files (literally files in your normal filing system) or even more simply facts books (summaries on sheets in a loose-leaf binder). In addition, you could also set up a 'clippings' file to contain the news stories and articles that you find about your products, markets and competitors.

The first facts (i.e. those usually the easiest to find and often the most important) typically relate to product/company performance. In recent years they have generally been handled by computer. They should include accurate sales data – split by product and by region – and it should even be possible to obtain up-to-date information via your own personal computer. Regrettably, even if the system is near-perfect, it is likely to take account of only those transactions that result in the organisation actually completing a sale; it is unlikely to record those – just as important – that are lost!

Even so, there may still be masses of data to record and analyse, and a very practical device that can assist you in organising this data is what is called 'ABC analysis'. This could not be simpler in principle. When you (or, more likely, your computer) are listing the results of any analysis, you just print the output in descending order of importance. In this way, the key items are always at the top and receive your immediate attention; conversely, the minor ones are at the bottom where it does not matter if they are ignored. This may sound trivial, but by itself it may revolutionise your view of the world. No longer will those customers, and products, whose name starts with the letter 'A' dominate your life! Thus where, for instance, a listing will typically be in terms of volume (or value) of sales, the highest volume (and hence most important) customers will be at the top of the list and the many low-volume customers at the bottom; and, as the top 20% of customers on such a list are likely to account for 80% of total sales, this approach can, in effect, be used to reduce the data to be examined by a factor of five.

This reference to 80% and 20% brings us to what may be the most powerful concept of all in management theory: the 80:20 Rule (also mentioned in Chapter 2), which has been in use for more than a century. First enunciated by an Italian, Pareto (hence its alternative title, the Pareto Rule), it is just as relevant today. It is still one of the most productive tools, and one of the few general ones that can be applied to almost any marketing situation. It simply recognises that the distribution of potential, be it in terms of products or customers or whatever, will almost inevitably be skewed. Some of these will be more important – heavy users say – than others, and some will be *much* more important. That the typical skew is so large that 80% of sales, say, comes from 20% of customers (and conversely that 80% of customers contribute no more than 20% of turnover) may come as a surprise; but has been borne out by countless practical examples. Its power comes from the fact that it enables you to concentrate your resources on just that 20%, confident that these are the important ones, responsible for 80% of your business – and you can safely limit any investment put into the other 80%.

Activity 3.2

Take the list of your customers or, failing that, your products or services, and list them in order of importance. How well does the 80:20 Rule apply? Does this change your opinion of the customers (or products or services) in question?

Sales reports

Another potentially invaluable source of information available at the desk is the reports sent in by the salesforce, although in this case it is likely to take the form of words rather than figures. If they are doing their job properly, and it has to be admitted that is a big 'if' in the case of badly managed sales teams, their reports will provide revealing insights into what makes individual customers, and the overall market, tick. The reports should also give advance notice of what your competitors are doing. So it is worth treating these reports like the gold-dust they really are!

➡ EXTERNAL 'DESK' RESEARCH

As the title of this section suggests, such research uses data that does not come from within the organisation, and for which the main source is published data (in its widest sense), often referred to as secondary data (because it has been generated in response to someone else's questions). Once suitable data has been located, its handling follows the same processes as for internal data. It is the 'finding' that is different.

The widest-ranging source of published data (on everything from details of ancient civilisations through to the latest stock market prices) is usually a library, typically a public reference library, either in paper or electronic form. Reference libraries, which are usually part of a local authority's central library, will hold stocks of books on a wide range of subjects. More important, though, is that these libraries have access to national libraries. As a result, if you can find sufficient information to specify the book (usually author, title, publisher and date of publication – though often just the author and title may suffice), it can usually be retrieved from this source. I consult literally hundreds of books (and articles) in this way each year.

For data located in journals, often specialist periodicals, the best source may be one of the more specialised libraries, such as those run by trade associations. The most important directories will also be available in your central library; but, again, the more specialised ones may only be found in those of trade associations. National and local government departments and agencies are often major providers of data, especially to support specific initiatives – but they may still be useful for other purposes. Another of the best sources of data, not least the 'informal' data acquired during conversations at meetings, is that of trade associations. There is usually a fee for membership, but this is frequently very good value in terms of what may be learned from these sources.

A growing amount of information is now being made available on the Internet, although it may be difficult to find amidst a mass of other material. As it is free (apart from any chargeable access or telephony costs), it is worth a try. As the 'search engines', the Web services that offer to locate data for you, seem to change almost on a weekly basis, I will not attempt to tell you exactly how to use these; but it is important that you *do* use them, and they really are easy to use.

Finally, the most prevalent, but unrecognised, source of external data for all managers (and the one that covers the widest perspective) is that of the news media (especially the morning newspapers and the television news and current affairs programmes). The amount of information that these provide is probably vastly greater than that received from any other source, albeit that the coverage is so much wider. Ideally, a number of newspapers should be read (even if only occasionally – and then only an additional weekend newspaper) to judge the bias each almost inevitably imparts to even the simplest news item.

➡ SURVEY RESEARCH

The next stage, having found out as much as you can from existing information, may be to undertake your own specific and direct (primary) research. Although you will appreciate that many of my earlier comments about listening to customers apply equally here, this investigation is likely to be more formally structured, and more comprehensive in its nature. The end result, from a number of interviews, say, should offer a meaningful explanation rather than a disconnected series of anecdotes. At this stage, therefore, I will divert into the rather academic world of market research. In this context there are two main approaches: qualitative research, which paints a general shape of what is happening (without any numbers), and quantitative research, which takes this outline picture and fills in the detail with statistics as – for instance – to how many customers fit into a certain marketing category.

Qualitative research

Much of the research, probably most of it, falls into this area. In industrial markets, for instance, there may be so few customers that in-depth interviews – unstructured interviews taking literally hours to complete, which are the staple diet of industrial market researchers – are the only way of conducting research. The high cost of employing the very skilled interviewers needed is justified by the importance of these customers to your business. One caveat: making sense of these interviews requires a great deal of skill, so you are quite dependent on the expertise and knowledge of the researcher.

In industrial markets where there are more customers, and more generally in consumer markets, the equivalent type of research is the focus group. You gather together half-a-dozen or so typical customers or prospects in a group and you get them to talk – freely – about the ideas you are investigating. The reason for this is not the efficiency of asking questions of six people at a time (although that helps) but is because this process seems to unlock the deeper thoughts that ordinary interviews miss. It may seem nonsensical, that people are more willing to talk about their innermost thoughts in a group of strangers, but experience shows that it works – they are willing to 'come out' in this way on the most intimate of subjects!

In this way, you can explore, for example, the real dimensions that may apply to the market segment you want to penetrate. You start them talking, or at least a trained moderator does (for, once more, this needs a very skilled touch if the moderator is not to impose his or her own views), and listen. Audio or video taping the debate for later analysis is essential. As a result, focus groups are very much the domain of the expert; beware the charlatans who might prey on you – and be certain to take up references! Beware, also, those who tell you this is a cheap form of research that will answer all your questions; in most cases it should usually be just the starting point for quantitative research.

One further caveat: it is far too easy to select, from the range of views expressed by the participants, just those comments that seem to support your own prejudices. These will, no doubt, leap from the report when you read it, where other less supportive comments will disappear; so listen to the analysis of the experts, not to your own prejudices.

If your organisation uses such focus groups, try to view a tape from one of these; most are now captured on video.

Quantitative research

As indicated above, the key to sound research is usually quantifica-
tion, so that you know how many customers fall into a particular
category, say. Not least – in the context of the previous caveat –
this stops you from just using the fuzzy results that come out of
qualitative research to bolster your own prejudices!

In textbooks, this topic often takes most of a whole (long)
chapter by itself; it certainly does in my own writings. In essence,
though, you take the questions that have emerged from the focus
groups – for these, rather than any answers, are the most useful
outcome – and use them as the basis for a formal questionnaire.
Yet again, writing such questionnaires is the province of the
experts because amateurs ask questions that result in biased
answers – too often just the ones they are wanting to hear! Then
you pose these questions to a sample of customers or prospects: the
survey itself. Again, I will not get into the niceties of statistically
sound sampling; suffice it to say that by questioning a few hundred
customers you can get results that are as accurate as if you had
asked a few hundred thousand – or everyone!

The traditional way of carrying out such a survey is to let loose
an army of interviewers to knock on doors or to accost people in
the street. There are advantages in such an approach, as long as the
interviewers are well supervised (which, be warned, they sometimes aren't). They need to be because quite complex questions can
be asked, and the interviewers have the respondents' 'body-langua-
ge' to help them understand their replies. But it can be very
expensive; so, despite everything you imagined, it is not very often
used.

Much more likely is the mailed questionnaire, which is used by
many more organisations, including those in industrial markets,
and where the questions are sent by post. Many academics deride
this approach as being inaccurate, but my own evidence is that –
given the correct design – it needn't be; and it is much, much
cheaper, so you can't offer the cost of the research as an excuse for
not finding out what your customers really think! But it does have
its limitations: the questions can't be complex, and the questionnaire has to be short; and you don't have body language to help
you out. Telephone surveys lie somewhere between the two

approaches, and are now the staple diet of political pollsters because they get the results back so fast.

Analysis

There is a wide range of bewildering computer analyses that can now be applied to the results. My advice is quite simply to look at the raw results, the simple tables of how many customers fall into each category. If the answers do not leap out at you from these, then the sophisticated computerised analyses are probably reporting results that lie on the borderline – and do you want to bet your money on such thin evidence? The exceptions are those areas, such as segmentation, where factor and cluster analyses are needed to find the groups. Here, the only advice is to find yourself a statistician you really trust!

The report

Most managers are poorly trained in the skills needed to make sense of the reports which emerge from these processes. As a result, they tend to read the related conclusions uncritically, accepting (or sometimes rejecting) them at their face value, and usually on the basis of what they think of the researcher presenting them or whether or not the results confirm their own existing prejudices.

Perhaps the most important question, but the one that is least often asked, is how *reliable* is the work. What weight can be put on the results, on the judgement of the researchers, and (probably even more importantly) on the experts who are likely to be recommending some form of action to be taken on the basis of the findings. Most research reports contain bias, conscious or unconscious. It is very difficult for even the most professional researcher to remove all of his or her biases; and you would be wise to assume that the material still contains such elements of distortion. In detail, therefore, the various stages should be as follows:

- **Summary:** the first element that should be read. This will provide the context for understanding the detailed results. It should, though, be read in that spirit, not as a list of proven facts, and certainly not (if the research is important) instead of the detailed material.

- **Detailed results**: these should be fully examined, preferably by looking at the original analyses (tables) as well as the written interpretation since any interpretation distances you from the facts. They should, once more, be examined critically. Do you agree with what the researcher has deduced from them? There is no reason that any researcher should be more capable than you in terms of this analysis. He or she, it is true, should be more experienced in the marketing research techniques involved, but you should be more experienced in the field being researched.

- **Think out your own summary**: only then can you think through (and put down on paper) what the key results are in terms of what affects your own work. It is a long process; but if the research is worthwhile, the effort you give to it should match its importance – and, hopefully, your subsequent decisions will be correspondingly better informed.

Activity 3.5

Try to get hold of a market research report that has been prepared for your organisation. Then do exactly what I recommended in the bullet points above. Can you then make sense of the reports?

➡ WALKABOUT

The penultimate technique in this section has the simplicity that is the hallmark of the Japanese, and it is their favourite approach: the walkabout. The power of the Japanese approach to marketing research is no more than going out and about, where the action is on the product or service in question, and experiencing what is happening. In particular, they meet their customers and distributors and talk through, at length, what is important to them.

It has none of the statistical validity that survey research enjoys, and that even desk research can often lay claim to. Yet better than anything else it conveys the flavour, the *essence*, of what is being studied. If you want to understand Toyota, you can spend months of desk research reading the hundreds of papers that have been written about its efficiency, or (as I have done) you can spend half a day watching the confident grace with which the workers on its production lines assemble cars. The essence is experience: assimilating what is happening and what is really important to the product or service.

Using this very crude approach, the Japanese achieve spectacular understanding – the key to effective research – of what is happening in their markets. Perhaps even more important, they then act upon this. So much research in the West just ends up lost in a filing cabinet. If you don't do anything as a result of your research, it has been wasted!

Activity 3.6

Do such a walkabout! Talk, if you are allowed to, to some customers. Try and see the world, and your organisation, through their eyes. *Become* a customer; phone in as if you are one, and be prepared to be horrified at your treatment!

➡ USING YOUR RESEARCH RESULTS

The walkabout introduces the final technique, which (for those managers that can use it) brings together all the search data in the most practical form possible. For many, if not most, managers, marketing research data remains as so much impersonal data lying on hundreds of pages of tables in dusty files. Just a few managers, however, bring it alive by assimilating it into their everyday view of their business life. They build an *inner* model of the customers they are dealing with. In this way, using the data you have received, you should try to synthesise a multidimensional picture of your typical customer, and then assimilate it into yourself, almost as if absorbing it by osmosis through your skin.

Needless to say, the technique of walkabout is the most useful of all in this process, because it gives the best 'feel' for what the key elements are. It is rather like the actor who uses 'the Method' to bring the character he is to play inside himself. He does not play the part, he *lives* it. In similar fashion, the synthesising manager should live the part of the customer. The great benefit of this is that the manager does not have to search through the vast collections of data to know what the customer's reaction would be to any of the several dozen decisions that may be made in a day – that would be unproductively time consuming and is precisely why the research results gather dust. Instead, he or she can draw upon their inner model to instinctively 'feel' what the customer's response will be.

Chapter 4
What product? What service?

Now we know who the customer is, let's look at what we think our product or service might be. In this chapter, though, we are going to be talking a lot about the product or the service, so let us – for the time being at least – get rid of the need monotonously to repeat the phrase 'product or service'. So I will just use the term 'product', but, where I do, it will apply equally to the product *or* service being offered; and, for the record, it will apply equally to the not-for-profit sectors as much as the commercial ones – as happens throughout this book.

The first point that has to be made is that, while you might now expect it to be sometimes difficult to define exactly who the customer is, surely at least you should know what your own product is! After all, it is your organisation making the product, and who could know better? By now you will probably anticipate my answer: the customer. You will know what goes into the product, but that is not all that makes up what is often called the 'product package'. Even if you are the exception and do know in general what it means to a customer, you may still be missing some of the richness inherent in the product package.

Let's take the example of the humble can of baked beans. The beans themselves are, of course, important. However, no matter how carefully selected the varieties may be or how carefully nurtured under ideal conditions, they are still just beans. Add the sauce, made from a secret recipe, and you have rather more – an appetising dish. But it still needs the tin can before you can sell it in the supermarket, a classic piece of packaging and yet something that almost everyone only sees as taking up space in the dustbin.

Without it you wouldn't be able to ship these ready-prepared beans to the families who want them, but such packages are no longer just containers for they are used to make important statements about the brand. As it so happens, in the case of the brand leader, Heinz, the statement on the baked bean can is very simple – a giant logo (reminding us of just how powerful the brand can be!) For some products, though, the packaging can even be the most important element, and may cost more than the contents. The classical example is perfume, where the package has to convey the right feel of luxury. Here we are already starting to look at the psychological aspects of the overall package. But there may also be service elements; not many in the case of baked beans, but possibly the careful attention of the sales assistant in the selected outlets where the perfume is sold, and in the case of complicated equipment there will be all the service engineers and support centres.

So we are already building a picture of a rich mixture of tangible product elements with intangible services, all overlaid with psychological overtones. To help bring some semblance of order to this picture, it is often depicted as an onion (see Figure 4.1), with the core product at the centre, various layers of services and intangible psychology building up around it, and usually, the image (developed by the advertising) as the outer layer.

The image may be the most important of all. In the case of baked beans, the purchaser may not want to buy the humble bean but to create a happy family – indeed, the perfect one shown in the commercials! You love your children and you want to show them this; and what better way to do this than buying Heinz. All of this built on that humble bean, but you should be able to see just how rich some product packages may be! Sometimes this comes about by happy accident, but more often it comes from hard effort of a brand-management team. The key message, for marketers, is that they must understand what makes up the *whole* rich package they are dealing with.

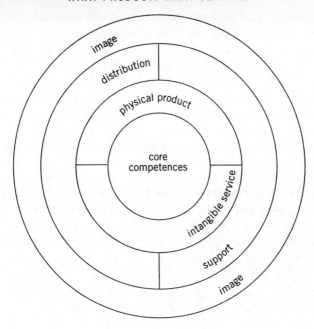

Figure 4.1: The onion layers of the 'product package'

What makes up the whole product package that your organisation is marketing? What are the physical and intangible elements of the product? What are the psychological overtones that give it its distinctive character (image)?

The product chapters of marketing textbooks are a veritable cornucopia of wonderful ideas and theories related to assessing products and services. I will briefly look at a number of these, partly because they help to pose some of the questions that need to be asked, but mainly because other people – especially marketing people – will talk to you in these terms, and you will not want to seem ignorant. In addition, they will probably ask you to believe that these ideas offer the infallible answers you need, and you had better understand why they almost certainly do not!

➡ VALUE CHAINS

Coming at the product from a different direction, it is now quite trendy to talk about marketing adding customer value. More basically, reflecting a focus on costs, in his book *Competitive Advantage* Michael Porter described the 'value chains' that build up the overall added value. In essence, you can look at your product in terms of all the things that go into it: the raw materials and components bought in from outside, the labour used inside the factory to make the product, the overheads associated with this production, and the cost of the warehousing and distribution. Each of these represents part of the value chain; the value that is added as the product moves through production and to the customer. The idea of value-chain analysis is that you can optimise each of these steps, to optimise the overall performance of the organisation.

In this context, an especially powerful tool is 'sensitivity analysis'. All you need do is look at a particular element of the value chain and notionally add 10% to its cost, and – using a computer spreadsheet – see how this affects the overall total cost. In this way, you might find that increasing the cost of a component increases overall costs by 1%, but increasing the labour used on that component might add 2%; so it could be worthwhile redesigning the component, even at extra cost, to reduce the labour cost. In essence, sensitivity analysis allows you to zero in on the areas where you can most effectively reduce costs.

The problem is that, as we saw, a product is generally much more complex than this approach allows for – and most of the intangible (service) elements are not susceptible to such sensitivity analyses; much of marketing is an art rather than a science! What you do about the image elements of a brand moves the whole process into the theatre of magic! So value-chain analysis is a nice idea, and offers wonderful exam questions for students and may even be useful for some manufacturing processes, but like much of the theory thrown into marketing it is not of very much practical help to most organisations.

➡ CORE COMPETENCES

'Core competences' is another piece of jargon that you may hear bandied around – indeed, you have already seen it used in the earlier 'onion' diagram (Figure 4.1) but this may have rather more validity. It arises from a process that looks at your product, or more typically your whole organisation, to see what special skills it holds – the special things it can do that no one else can do, or that it can do better than anyone else. Your organisation might be able to machine parts more accurately than anyone else, so perhaps you should invest in even better machine tools to retain your place as a leading provider to the aircraft manufacturing industry. Or maybe it is the skills of the workforce that result in this accuracy, so you should train them or pay them more so you don't lose them. Or, as a bank, it may be your coverage of the marketplace – in olden days the number of high street branches but now more likely to arise from the power of your computer technology.

The point of all this is that the core competences can be quite different for different firms, even ones in the same industry. The importance is that you recognise what are *your* core competences. This is not quite as simple as it seems: most organisations have a good idea of what they think they do best but, as always, this may not be the same as the customer's view of their virtues. In addition, the view you will have, along with that of the customers, will be historically based; it will reflect what has been important in the past. But this view may not be true for the future, and so it is important also to ask yourself what competences will be needed in ten years' time, say.

| Activity 4.2 |

Try to work out what are your organisation's core competences. What sets it apart from other organisations? This is not an easy question to answer, so try initially to look at it from a number of perspectives:

- **your own view**: the easy one: what do you think are the organisation's special skills?

- **your customers' view**: how might your customers answer the same question?

- **your competitors' view**: this is a quite enlightening question in its own right.

- **ten years' ahead**: maybe the most enlightening view of all is to ask yourself how you might answer the question a decade from now.

Then ask the same question(s) about your own group's core competences.

➡ PRODUCT LIFE CYCLE

Product Life Cycle is possibly the best known, and most frequently quoted, piece of marketing theory. It simply says that a product is born, then grows to maturity and finally dies as its usefulness comes to an end. The power lies in its analogy with the human life cycle, which we know all too well, and it does have some useful aspects. Not least it underlines the potential *mortality* of any product, and in many fields it is a salutary reminder of what happens if you leave your product unchanged for long periods. What worked for yesterday's markets, and perhaps for today's as well, may not meet the changed needs of tomorrow's markets. So you had better understand what lies in store.

In essence, the Product Life Cycle (PLC) can be split into three main phases: growth, maturity and decline. As can be seen, from the diagram in Figure 4.2, it is often split into more portions – here, the growth phase is added to the initial introduction – depending upon what the academics are trying to show.

In the first of these stages – growth – the PLC can remind you of what we saw earlier when we looked at diffusion, namely how typical growth starts slowly and then accelerates until it plateaus at maturity. Then comes maturity when the product makes all the profits everyone hopes for, but, bad news, then comes the decline and the product is no more!

So what are the problems? Well, the main problem is that we

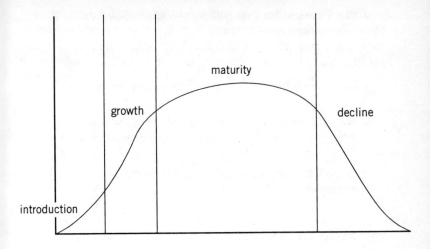

Figure 4.2: A product life cycle

should not really be talking about a product; as we have seen, the real focus is the brand. It is true that, under the umbrella of that brand, products, or at least product features, come and go, but that is under the control of the brand manager and the PLC does not really describe this man-made process. But in the case of a successful brand, which is where you should place your money, the PLC is effectively infinite, with the brand always in the mature phase. Unsuccessful brands rapidly die, but then you don't need the PLC to tell you this.

My research shows that, in most stable markets, the brand leaders have lives that run into decades, and occasionally into centuries. Where most marketing plans run for no more than three years, this means the PLC is irrelevant in terms of practice. I like to give the example of being the brand manager for dinosaurs. Should you worry about the decline of your brand? It will surely come, but perhaps not for another 150 million years! Well, something like this happens with most large brands. It may not be 150 million years, but in practical terms it may as well be. We need something, therefore, that works with the featureless part of the PLC, the mature phase. Otherwise, nice idea, nice exam question, but not much use! My answer is in Figure 4.3: the Competitive Saw.

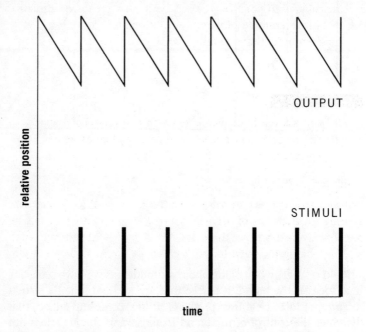

Figure 4.3: The Competitive Saw

The steady state of the mature brand is not, in fact, steady! Its position is affected by the positive stimuli we regularly apply: advertising and promotional campaigns, product improvements, sales drives etc. Each time we improve our competitive effort in this way, it improves product performance and ultimately gains brand share. Thereafter, however, it loses share again; as the competitor campaigns have the opposite effect or the market steadily drifts away from us. The mature brand is, thus, constantly under opposing forces, and the 'Competitive Saw' of Figure 4.3 reminds us that we need to *maintain* our activities if the brand is not to be swamped by competitive pressures and market changes. In theory, we could work out exactly what was the impact of each of the elements involved so that we could optimise our performance, but I have only ever been able to do that once in my life. It made literally millions of pounds for the organisation I then worked for, but the circumstances were exceptional and regrettably not repeatable! In practice, you see, with very few exceptions this Saw is only a reminder of what not to do! But, as such, it is a very valuable reminder that you must continue to maintain your brand, rather than milk it.

Activity 4.3

All I can ask you to do here is to watch how your organisation's fortunes (its sales performance, say) come and go as its promotional programmes (or new products) impact them.

Which nicely brings me on to the part of the PLC that can be positively dangerous to your organisation's health. If you are waiting for the signs of decline, the end of the product's life, you are bound one day to see them. We are all very good at seeing what we are looking for; even in the flimsiest of (false) evidence! Then you will put in place all the things that are recommended for a declining brand, and you will most likely kill a perfectly healthy one! The reality is that you don't have to go out looking for dying brands – they tell you so very clearly themselves!

The Boston Matrix

Which in turn leads on to one of the most famous, and to my mind most infamous, theories, a perennial favourite of the marketing textbooks. This is a four-box matrix developed a few decades ago, when conglomerates were in fashion and proving difficult to control. The Boston Consulting Group quite reasonably at that time developed the device as a means of predicting the cash flows of business units on the basis of their market shares in expanding markets. Unfortunately, it only worked in rapidly expanding markets, greater than 10% per annum (as were the high-tech markets at the time it was developed), and even then only for brand leaders.

The potential disaster came when the bowdlerisers got there hands on it. It was turned into a device for predicting the overall performance of *any* product, not just the cash flow arising from business units with brand leaders, and the market growth aspects were conveniently forgotten. Worst of all, the careful plotting of actual performance figures was thrown out in favour of four stereotypes (see Figure 4.4) known as 'stars', 'cash cows', 'dogs' and 'problem children'.

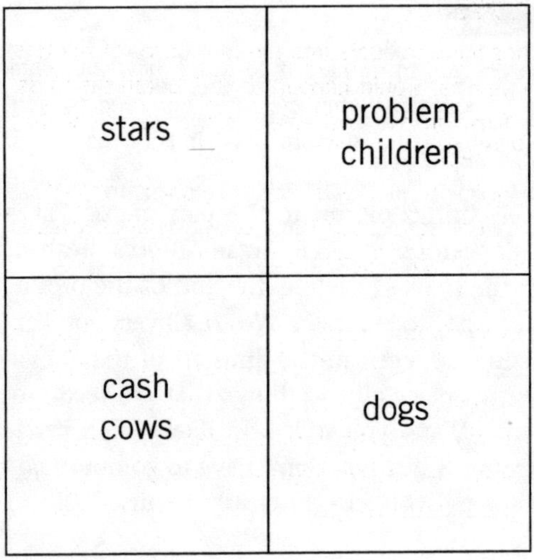

stars	problem children
cash cows	dogs

Figure 4.4: The Boston Matrix

Thus, according to these stereotypes, you launch a new product, which becomes a 'problem child' until you can make it into a 'star', which in turn finally makes the grade as a 'cash cow' before, in turn, ultimately ending its life as a 'dog'. The relationship to the PLC is clear. The key link, though, is between the cash cows, which are milked of all their profits, and the stars, which receive the resulting investments needed to fuel their growth. This is definitely not what the Boston Consulting Group intended, and is positively *dangerous* if used for the future of an organisation.

Indeed, it pushes you in exactly the opposite direction to the one you should be following. Instead of maintaining the mature brands, the cash cows, so that they will continue to produce profits almost for ever, you are supposed to milk them, accepting that they will soon become dogs and die! New products (stars) are, as we shall see, quite important – but nowhere as near as important as your profit earners.

Activity 4.4

Try putting your products into the four boxes of the Boston Matrix. Then think what would happen to your organisation as a result of milking those in the cash cows box so severely that they died within the next year!

The concept of the Boston Matrix (along with the PLC to which it relates) can be seductively simple, but hopefully this exercise will show you just how dangerous it can be!

I have taken some time to demolish this particular piece of theory because it is a good example of what may face you when you talk to marketing people. It should be obvious that – in the cash cows form – it is nonsense; but it is taught in every business school I know! Fortunately, as my research shows, most managers have the good sense to ignore it!

The Three-Choice Box

If you must use a matrix to help you sort out the options available to you, please use the General Electric (GE) Matrix, which is the one most often used by the strategists in larger organisations, or my derivative from it. The factors that the GE Matrix plots are more 'intuitive' than those used by the Boston Matrix. Thus, the vertical axis simply plots the 'product/market attractiveness' – in other words, how worthwhile (or otherwise) the business is. The horizontal axis covers 'business strength/competitive position' – what the organisation's competitive advantage is in each. In its correct usage, calculating these positions can be a sophisticated process, and so look up the details in a specialist textbook if you want to use this approach with the correct precision! What seems to be even more complex is that it is a 3 × 3 matrix.

The whole approach can, however, be considerably simplified without losing its inherent value, so my version – 'The Three-Choice Box' – is given in Figure 4.5. This simpler version offers a more immediate picture that nevertheless still retains the flexibility and intuitive practicality of the original. It has the great virtue that it brings out the many subjective decisions that lie beneath the surface of the original GE Matrix. Both the attractiveness of the product/market and the strength of the business are clearly subjective (albeit informed) values. It also highlights the fact that there is a spectrum of outcomes.

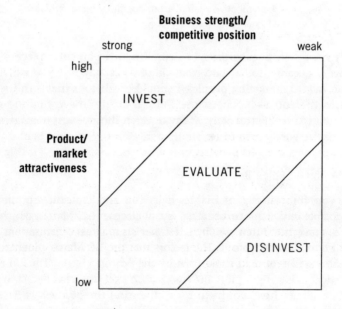

Figure 4.5: The Three-Choice Box

➡ NEW PRODUCTS

Much of the emphasis of academic marketing theories is on new products. After all, in our rapidly changing society, we all need new products, don't we? Whilst I would not deny their importance and certainly would not dissuade you from developing them, you *must* put them in perspective. When you say 'new products' to people, it conjures up the romantic vision of the white-coated scientist toiling in his lab to create the next leap forward, the drug that will save the world. Although there may be many such dedicated researchers, and even some successful ones, in reality almost all R&D is focused on the improvement – the redevelopment – of *existing* products, exactly as it should be. The outcome is, for instance, the 'new blue whitener' you find in your detergent. But that's where the greatest part of the business is to be found, and certainly by far the greatest profits. So, constantly improving your product to match changing needs or competitor moves is exactly what our Competitive Saw (Figure 4.3) demands.

The Ansoff Matrix

In the context of new product development in general, another matrix – again another favourite with the academics though this time with rather better justification – is the matrix based on Igor Ansoff's ideas, as shown in Figure 4.6.

The top-left quadrant is what we have already been talking about: redevelopment of existing products in the existing market; to improve market penetration of existing markets – taking business from competitors – or to generate more usage by persuading existing users to buy more. The essence of this, as I have said previously, is keeping up with, and preferably being ahead of, both your competitors and your customers. The upper-right quadrant is new products for existing markets. This is what marketing people typically think of as 'new product development'; and we will return to notion this shortly.

	Existing product	**New product**
Existing market	MARKET PENETRATION	PRODUCT DEVELOPMENT
New market	MARKET DEVELOPMENT	DIVERSIFICATION

Figure 4.6: The Ansoff Matrix

Then, bottom left, there are existing products moving into new markets. This may result from a major repositioning, as Lucozade successfully did when moving from being the drink for sick invalids to the one for very healthy athletes; or it may more likely arise from a physically new market – typically as export business. Finally, there is the dreaded word of diversification. Once very popular, spreading your risks across a number of markets, it now flies in the face of the 'focus' demanded of efficient organisations. But it does still happen, and if it does my advice is to 'buy' an organisation – by acquisition or merger – that already has expertise in the new market, for the risks faced by inexperienced market entrants can be horrendous.

Indeed, the hidden – and very important – message of the Ansoff Matrix is that risk increases the further you get away from your home base at the top left, and it usually increases to unacceptable levels at the bottom right! The general advice is to stick with what you know.

Developing new products

Even so, there is a lot of romance, and some practical advantage, in developing new products. After all, these do from time to time manage to overturn existing brand positions, albeit far less frequently than people suppose. So you had better be prepared for the possibility. In fact, if you are brand leader, you probably won't want to take the risk of bringing in a really new product, since it may destabilise a market where you are doing nicely. But you need to have one on the stocks ready for when someone else brings in their own challenger.

There are all sorts of creative-thinking techniques that are recommended for devising really new products. But the reality is that the successful ones usually emerge from nowhere. I well remember a presentation I heard by the marketing director of a multinational company, in which he carefully explained all the classical processes they had followed in the development and launch of a new product – all straight from the marketing textbook. Later, he privately admitted to me that the idea had come to him while he was mowing the lawn; but hadn't said this since the marketers in his audience wouldn't have liked it!

So, in practice there are just two necessities with new products. The first is that, when the idea comes to you or is brought to you by one of your staff, you must have a sufficiently open mind that you can recognise it. Sony has an enviable reputation for new product development, but this came about because its legendary CEO had a superb nose for recognising potential; and 3M have built a similar reputation, in their case as a management team, on much the same basis. Then, secondly, you must commit all the considerable resources needed to bring it to the market, and that will usually represent a major investment. This brings into play the opposite aspect, which is needed to safeguard the organisation against expensive mistakes – as, for instance, the Concorde airliners proved to be. This is that new products must be sieved through a rigorous screening process to ensure that they are not just technically brilliant but that they genuinely meet the needs of the market.

The conventional stages of such a screening programme look thus:

- **Strategic screening**: does it fit with what your expertise and resources can deliver, and with the markets you serve?
- **Concept test**: even before you start laboratory work on development, does the *idea* appeal to customers?
- **Product development**: the traditional R&D stage.
- **Product test**: does the product meet with approval from the customers?

Only then do you launch the new product. There used to be another stage, in the gentler-paced days of my youth, which was that of a test market (one ITV television area, say) to see if the customers would actually be likely to buy the product. This is rare these days because, when markets are moving so fast, it also tells your competitors exactly what you are up to, and there is then every chance they will get a similar product into the national market *before* you. And the first product into a new market usually ends up as the brand leader. So you must grit your teeth and risk everything on an unknown product in a national launch.

It is even worse than that, since you now may have to undertake a *global* launch. Time was when you could try it out on your home turf and then roll it out country by country – but no more: once again, your competitors will get there first. This means that important new product launches, on a global scale, can cost hundreds of millions of pounds and the risks can be very high. Intel had to launch its original Pentium chip worldwide in this way, only to find a bug that cost literally hundreds of millions of dollars to issue a recall and rectify; but, even so, the investment was worthwhile, since it safeguarded its effective monopoly.

Activity 4.5

How good is your own organisation at recognising new products? How does your organisation strategically screen its new products? How effective is this process?

➡ MARKET PENETRATION VERSUS 'SKIMMING'

Your aim nowadays is, as we have seen, to get new products (and even changes to existing products) into the market very rapidly. You achieve this by investing, often heavily, in promotions, but particularly in low prices. Indeed, the decisions here are encapsulated in the strategic decisions between market penetration (which is what I have been describing) and 'skimming'.

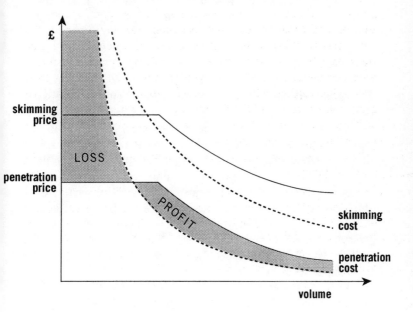

Figure 4.7: Skimming v penetration

By setting a low penetration price, as shown in Figure 4.7, you can dominate the market. It may cost large amounts of money in the short term, but it can offer something like a monopoly position in the longer term.

The alternative, which was widely followed in the old days and is still followed by smaller organisations in less competitive markets, is 'skimming'. In this case, the introductory price is set high, at a premium, to take advantage of the uniqueness and scarcity of the new product. The price is only reduced as sales grow and as necessary to match competitive moves. This optimises short-term profits, and may optimise profit overall if the competitors are weaker than you. But unfortunately they all too often are not; and you risk losing your position as brand leader.

Activity 4.6

Which approach – penetration or skimming – does your own organisation favour for new product launches? What are the strategic implications of this approach?

➡ PRICING

This nicely introduces us to a topic that typically justifies a separate chapter in marketing textooks and a number of chapters in economics books: pricing. The reason that, in this book, it represents just *part* of the present chapter is twofold. The first is that a separate chapter would perpetuate the myth that (low) pricing is much more important than any other single factor in achieving success, and that is just not true. The second is to emphasise that it is just one aspect of the product package, and should be determined by the overall positioning of the brand! Indeed, once you have determined the brand position – as we saw earlier – you should have decided the whole range of parameters applying to it, *including price*.

In part, this overemphasis comes from the classical economics developed many decades ago when price *was* the only variable. Then price was supposed to be set by the 'laws of supply and demand', best illustrated by the famous graph in Figure 4.8. The correct (equilibrium) price was achieved when supply matched demand, the only problem being that it usually proved impossible in practice to plot these nice curves. So, yet again, nice idea and good exam question, but no use!

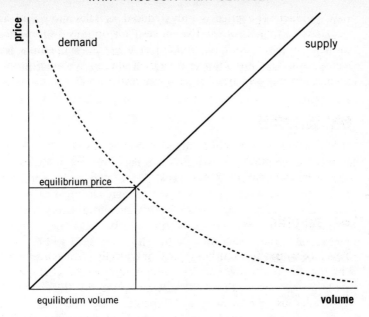

Figure 4.8: Product price equilibrium

Commodity or not?

In reality, there is one key question that you must ask yourself: is the product treated like a commodity, is price competition prevalent, and do your competitors cut prices savagely? If any of these is the case, you *must* match your competitors on price; otherwise you will soon be out of business. In fact, such markets are the despair of those working in them, for most suppliers in them lose money, and so you might be better out of them! Fortunately, such cut-price markets only represent something like one-tenth of all markets, although such is the fascination that they hold that most people think they are more widespread.

In most markets, however, sales are made on the basis of the attractiveness of the whole product package; and those with attractive packages overall can justify a price premium. This

premium, over the commodity price, is achieved because customers are convinced – for whatever reason – that they want your
brand more than others. Indeed, the highest price premium is
usually achieved by the brand leader – again against what most
people might expect. The exact reason for the premium is not
important, and it will vary from situation to situation; what is
crucial is that you recognise it as a possibility, and work to
maximise it.

If you avoid the pitfall of commodity pricing, most pricing then
turns out to be relatively simple. This is because most products or
services are either existing products with a known track record, or
are new products entering markets where there already are similar
products with known track records. This, therefore, signposts the
two main alternative methods, both of which tend to be scorned
by academics, but which (despite the shortcomings I will discuss
below) are eminently sensible.

Historical pricing

This is probably the most prevalent form of pricing, for good
reason: what the price has been in the past is, for most products or
services, the best starting point for what it should be in the future.
The caveat is that you must still be aware of how the price needs to
change to reflect the consumer's changing needs and different
competitive conditions. But most managers who are in touch with
their customers and markets should already be well aware of such
trends.

Competitive pricing

The one additional aspect that may modify historical pricing, and
may sometimes replace it (and always will in the case of new
products), is what competitors are doing. The positioning exercise,
of course, takes full account of the relative position with respect to
competitors, and so, once again, this should be a natural part of
the pricing process.

Cost-plus pricing

On the other hand, the other main approach, adding a fixed percentage (to show a 'profit') to costs, should *not* usually be considered. Costs should be minimised, but prices should be maximised, based upon what the customer is willing to pay – which is typically not directly linked to cost.

Activity 4.7

How does your organisation set its prices: on the basis of previous history, or on what the competition is doing, or in some other way? Is your organisation operating in a commodity market, with price cutting, or should it be able to get a price premium? Indeed, does it set its prices too low?

Chapter 5
Sales talk

We have found out what the customer wants and what we have to offer, hopefully matching these wants. So now let's now see how we tell the customers about what we have for them.

But, first, let me explain one further marketing concept you may come across: 'the marketing mix' or 'the four Ps'. We have seen how complex the product package may be, but many marketers like to integrate *all* the aspects of the brand, including promotion – the subject of this chapter and the next one. This integrated package is, overall, referred to as 'the marketing mix', and the term 'the four Ps' is usually offered as a simple (I would claim, as you will see later, simplistic) guide to its elements. These four Ps are: *product* and *price*, which we have already looked at, *promotion*, which we are about to explore, and *place*. This last category may offer a clue as to why I, and many other marketers, are dubious about the value of this approach. This rather oddball title of 'place' is included simply because it has a 'P' at the beginning of the word! In fact, it is a catch-all that sweeps up what is left over by a rather inadequate set of categories. In addition, the four Ps do not work well for services, so the predictable answer was to add another three: *people*, *process*, and *physical evidence*. But enough of this frivolity: like so many marketing gimmicks, this approach confuses and distracts more than it helps. So ignore it!

Back to the real world, and to 'promotion' in general. The term covers a very wide range of ways we can talk to customers. The easiest of these, and probably the most commonly used, is selling face to face. Your sales personnel meet with the customers, in their offices for industrial customers or in your shop for retail business, and talk to them face to face. But there are a whole range of other means of communication – for instance, at the other extreme, there is mass advertising. Where 'selling' involves just two people (the salesperson and the buyer) talking face to face, advertising talks to many – perhaps many millions – as a mass audience. This parallels the way that, earlier, we listened to large numbers with market research, although here we cannot just talk to a sample of them but must reach each and very one.

Clearly, the two extremes demand very different solutions. As I explained at the beginning of the book, this is not from choice – the perfect solution, in almost all cases, would be to send out a sales professional with every can of baked beans (though a lot of committed advertising folk would still have you believe that their commercials are better than any salesperson!). However, suppliers to the mass markets simply cannot afford face-to-face selling; advertising is their only option, which is why they have developed it into an art-form in their television commercials and their advertisements in newspapers and magazines.

Somewhere in between the two extremes sits 'direct marketing' – in the early days, 'direct mail', the junk-mail that landed on your doormat, but now the sophisticated promise of computerised database marketing! And there are others, from the immediacy of sales promotion, usually 'money-off ' to bring in very short-term business, to the long-term investment in public relations, building the image of the organisation through editorial comment in the media.

All of this is often referred to as the 'promotion(al) mix', which is a useful concept since it implies a carefully planned, integrated, mix of the separate elements of promotion so as to optimise the overall impact, rather than focusing exclusively on one or another – selling, say, for industrial goods, or advertising for consumer goods. Of course, certain of these elements will dominate in any marketing campaign: few consumer goods marketers would assume that they could only use sales personnel and few industrial CEOs would be happy to see all their marketing effort concentrated on advertising. But in almost all cases, a mix is used: sales teams persuade the supermarket owners to stock their mass-consumer goods, and merchandisers hand out samples to the consumers, and 'leads' (new prospects) are generated for sales teams by trade press advertising or mailshots.

There all sorts of clever ways of looking at the promotional mix; but in essence that is all it is – the most productive mix of the various forms of promotion open to you! So let's move along and look at some of the individual elements. We will start with selling, since – for most of us – this employs simple concepts that are easier to understand.

➡ SELLING: THE STRUCTURE

Selling has traditionally been seen as somewhat different from the other elements in the promotional mix, but that is a mistake – except for one thing. So let's get that genuine difference out of the way now. Selling is inherently about managing people, the customers at one extreme and the sales personnel (by their sales managers) at the other. So people management skills are very important. This contrasts with the other elements where (impersonal) resource management skills, and sometimes project management skills, are demanded; the consumer marketing manager is judged by how effectively he or she deploys the mass communication resources available.

Customer (account) management

The traditional view of selling has been that it is a 'professional' role (if even that) rather than a management one (where very few sales professionals formally manage teams of subordinates). In practice, much of the sales professional's role is actually concerned with *management*. The sales professional is typically solely responsible for his or her territory. He or she is responsible for everything that happens on this territory; for all activities, with the range of responsibilities (albeit on a smaller scale) comparable with those normally assumed by a brand manager or even by the chief executive of a subsidiary. In addition, every sales professional will have, to a greater or lesser extent, some organisational resources at his or her command (not least his or her own time) and also some

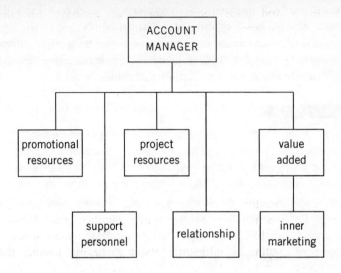

Figure 5.1: Account management

support resources (including service support, marketing support, and possibly even budgeted amounts of territory based promotional funding). All of these resources have to be managed in exactly the same way as the rest of the organisation's resources are managed by its team of managers.

It is also conventionally assumed that sales professionals do not manage people and, indeed, as mentioned earlier, very few actually have formal responsibility for subordinates. Yet, as you can see from the diagram in Figure 5.1, many salespersons indirectly control the activities of support personnel. What is more, they have to achieve this management control, often under difficult circumstances on customer premises, without any formal authority.

Above all, the sales professional manages the 'customer interface', that most important asset of any organisation, the relationship with the customer (and/or the customer organisation). This is the crucial 'goodwill' element of an organisation's work and demands a great deal of skill. It is also a role that contains many of the key elements of management in general, and is one from which other managers, perhaps including yourself, can learn some lessons (particularly about communication with other people).

Activity 5.1

Try to spend a day meeting customers with one of your organisation's sales personnel. This will not be easy to arrange, for most sales managers guard their fiefdoms more closely than Fort Knox protects its gold reserves. Nevertheless, if you can flatter your way through their defences, it will give you an invaluable insight into what makes marketing in general, and selling in particular, tick.

Territory management

The starting point for territory management is usually the salesperson's responsibility for their own small business – their 'territory'. For the past century or so, giving the salesperson (within limits) total responsibility for all activities taking place within that territory has provided the basic building block for *customer management by* that salesperson, and for *sales management of* that salesperson. Classically, territories have been geographically defined, not least because it is easy to define them by a simple line on a map; but they could alternatively be by industry or by product type. IBM, for instance, used all three of these. Most recently, as the emphasis on relationship management has developed, territories have tended to be instead a nominated (list of) customers.

Whatever the approach, sales people have a defined territory for which they bear total responsibility, and over which they have almost total authority. Although most sales managers would no doubt challenge this view, I have always found it useful to think of them operating on their territory in much the same way as the CEO operates within the overall organisation.

Activity 5.2

How is the territory of the salesperson (with whom you are

hopefully spending a day) defined? How do they then organise their work within it?

Customers and prospects

As we have seen, customers are, almost without exception, more productive than prospects; indeed, they are much more productive than many sales professionals (or their management) allow for. And if the organisation has previously offered good customer service, customers are already tied to it; competitors will have to justify breaking these links before they can even begin their own selling process. In such customers the organisation doesn't have to invest in the whole process of new business recruitment.

Yet too many sales personnel devote relatively too little time to customers than to their favourite prospects. They spend their time, unproductively, looking for new business, when they should be defending, and growing, their customer base. Instead, the rule should be to treat all such (marginal) prospects as outcasts.

So the first priority of any sales professional must be to allocate resources to the existing customers and, further, to differentiate between customers according to what they are worth. Some will be 'bankers' and will bring in a large part of the easy 80% of business we talked about when we looked at the 80:20 Rule. These investments must be protected, almost at any cost. Some, on the other hand, will be totally unproductive, demanding resource for little return; and in these cases the plan must be to contain the 'bleeding'.

At a lower level of priority, the key skill comes in being able to separate out the sheep from the goats amongst the prospects – those which form the 10% or so of prospects who will bring in at least 50% of the new business. No matter how much marginal prospects plead, no matter how much they befriend and flatter you, productive sales professionals have to be ruthless and refuse to fritter away resources on unproductive areas. So the true professional must insist that prospects (and customers) *prove* their good intentions. It is the reverse of what you might expect, but professional selling is as much about managing (and indeed rationing) scarce resources – and walking away from losers – as it is about winning friends and influencing people.

Activity 5.3

How do your sales personnel allocate their time between the various categories? Are they investing in productive customers, or frittering their efforts away on worthless new prospects? How could they better direct their energies?

People management

As we have seen, contact with the customer is not limited to that formally undertaken by sales personnel. There are a whole range of other people involved, on both sides. Thus, the salesperson may run a team of support personnel – most likely covering technical support but maybe also promotional and administrative support – with all the (indirect) people and resource management that this implies. Above all, the salesperson is (directly) responsible for managing the interface with the customer in general, and this involves many others (from telephone operators through to workers on the production lines).

Activity 5.4

What contact does your own group have with the organisation's customers? How well are these contacts managed?

➡ SELLING: THE PROCESS

We now look at the aspects of the selling process that help to generate real sales. These aspects may start with high-volume attempts to capture the attention of prospective customers, right down to face-to-face contact between a serious prospect and a sales professional.

Sales support

When – as usually happens – a sales campaign runs over a number of months, there can be a wide range of promotional activities involved – the 'promotional mix' is much richer than most people realise. The first stage is the generation of new leads – new business from existing customers or totally new prospects: The use of mailshots (or, sometimes, trade-press advertising) to generate these is fairly normal, and we shall look at this later in the chapter, as we will the telesales operations that are often used to follow up these initial enquiries.

Then there are the seminars used to 'process' these qualified leads further, in other words to screen them to see whether or not they are worth committing face-to-face sales personnel to – at the same time, by these seminars, starting a gentle process of persuasion. Prospects will come to a 'neutral' seminar, where they do not feel threatened, and the organisation will studiously avoid any sales contact. All of this leads up to that first call by a sales professional, confident that there is business to be had. These steps take time and money, but – as part of an overall programme of developing new business – they offer a much more productive approach than immediately committing valuable sales personnel whose time costs far more than most people realise (perhaps as much as several hundred pounds for each call).

Sales calls

If these preliminaries have taken place, by the time you get into the first face-to-face call you should find that much of the groundwork has already been done. To a degree the positive attitudes are already there – a great confidence booster for sales personnel and one that can almost carry them through to the close of a sale. Even so, despite all that some sales trainers claim, it usually takes a *number* of calls, often over a number of months, to get the business; and – again, against the popular image – much of selling demands a great deal of patience (not least for sales managers). But, whatever the timescales, it is certainly true that the more calls that are made, and more specifically the greater the number of prospects contacted, the greater will be the sales. This is often described in sales circles as the 'numbers game'.

Thus, reverting to the preliminaries, for every thousand mailshots sent out at the start of a campaign, there will be a certain percentage of returns that justify a sales professional calling personally; and telesales and cold calling will also generate proportional results. From these subsequent calls, a proportion will turn into serious prospects (some of whom will progress to demonstrations and proposals). And out of these serious prospects a proportion will place orders, and a proportion (hopefully a good proportion) will place those orders with the organisation undertaking these activities rather than with its competitors. This gradual whittling-down of numbers from a blanket mailshot to serious prospects is shown (with indicative proportions only) in Figure 5.2.

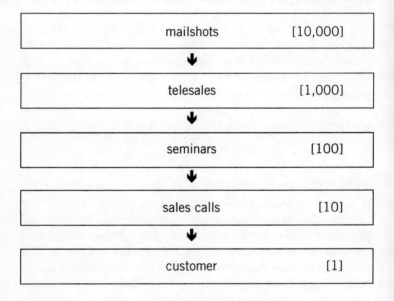

Figure 5.2: Finding serious prospects

Converting a good prospect into a customer requires all the skills a sales professional possesses, but it is a basic fact of the sales game that changing a number of prospects into sound business is just sheer hard work. The more mailshots sent out, the more teleselling done and the more cold calls made, the greater the raw material for the conversion process. The eventual outcome is almost directly proportional to the numbers that are fed in.

In contrast, one of the secrets of successful selling is based on exactly the opposite notion: that of discarding unproductive prospects as soon as possible, under the good old 80:20 Rule. This is why screening is so important at each level. Suprisingly, selling is a quite intensive investment process, so you need to weed out any prospects that will not justify such an investment before they waste too much of your time. The essence of good selling, in this context, is knowing when to say no – the very reverse of what sales people are usually taught!

Activity 5.5

Which of these aspects of sales support does your organisation engage in? How effectively does it use them? How are they used to filter out unproductive prospects?

Dialogue

I have said that this chapter is about 'talking' – telling the customer what you have got to offer – but, as you might by now expect, I will once again emphasise that it remains a *two-way* communication. That is an important lesson in selling, and it is also an important lesson in marketing in general, especially as it is an unexpected one. People think that once they have the sales message, all they need to do is shout it as loudly as they can! That couldn't be further from the truth. Even if you are advertising your product, you must seek feedback: is the advertising working; is the product (not least as conveyed by the adverts) really what the customers want; how could you do it all better?

But it is especially true for sales personnel. Even in the 'talking' phase, if I can call it that, you should probably spend more time *listening*. After all, the great benefit of selling face to face, denied to mass marketers, is that it is a dialogue! At each stage you should listen to your customers – and this applies just as much to those you deal with in your own job – so as to establish first of all that they have understood you (and, of course, that you have understood them) and then that they agree with what you are saying. Ultimately, you need to (genuinely) agree with them that what you are offering meets their needs; and, more subtly, that no competitor can better meet those needs. So, listen, listen, listen!

Closing a sale

Classically, sales campaigns have been split into a number of parts – often depicted by sales trainers as happening within just the *one* sales call needed to get the order. The most important of these parts are the two we have already looked at: listening (finding out what the customer wants) and talking (telling them what you have). I have already hinted at the next and final stage: that of agreement, although in sales parlance it is usually referred to as the 'close'. This assumes mythic proportions for many sales personnel, and is the one part of the overall process that departs from the concepts that I have been describing of dialogue and positive relationships, which in essence focus entirely on helping the customer.

Before describing the 'closing' stage, I will, however, throw in one rather strange element of sales training; that of objection handling. This is a set of 'pure' sales skills that encapsulates much of the traditional selling; and, as such, graphically illustrates many of the self-inflicted wounds that the 'profession' imposes on itself. It is supposed to enable the top salesmen to get round the objections of prospects to placing the business. Regrettably, to achieve this end, it demands much the same skills that a con-artist employs, thus creating the poor image that has haunted salesmen for decades. There is one further problem: there is almost no evidence that most customers actually deploy such objections – they are either confused (in which case you need to help them) or they are certain that your offer is not for them (in which case you should politely move on to something you can sell). I throw in this information because, unnecessary as such techniques may be, they can still loom large in the minds of many sales people. One of my more subversive pleasures was to teach my own customers about these 'objection handling' skills and then watch them destroy my competitors when they used them!

But back to the 'close', which is supposedly the subject of yet another set of 'pure' sales skills. In this case, there is some justification for having the skills, not for the customer – for these so-called 'skills' are ineffective in persuading them to place an order if they don't want to – but to boost the salesperson's own confidence. Indeed, this is often the one aspect that differentiates really successful sales people from their run-of-the-mill colleagues. The difference at this final stage is that it is no longer sufficient just to be a nice guy and help the customer. At the end of the day, you have to positively ask for the order. This is a much more aggressive act, and sometimes described (with some truth) as 'going for the jugular'.

This is quite difficult for most sales people; indeed, most of them hate this part of selling. Not merely is there the switch from the helpful to the (discreetly) aggressive, but their whole future seems to be about to be decided in a matter of minutes! They may often have been working on the sale for months, maybe even years, and then – in a matter of minutes – they will find out whether all that work has been wasted, whether they have been a success or failure, whether they will be able to face their management and their families. It is not surprising that the most frequent failure of sales professionals is to avoid asking for the order! But it has to be asked for, and most of the sales techniques – although claiming to influence the customer – are actually designed to make it easier for the salesperson to take that step and actually ask. Most sales managers quite simply make the threat of what will happen if they don't ask – an even more fearful prospect for the salesperson!

The element of personal 'danger' is very different from all other forms of product or brand promotion. As a marketing manager, you never have the same level of fear when your commercials are first aired; even if they ultimately prove to be a fiasco, the news is brought to you in small increments.

Activity 5.6

How do your sales people go about 'closing' their sales? How do they get over the psychological difficulties?

➡ RELATIONSHIP MANAGEMENT

Selling has traditionally been seen as a 'zero-sum game', where each of the participants can gain only at the expense of the other. This is now seen to be at odds with the trust needed to build *relationships* with customers of all types. Indeed, it is now widely recognised that the most productive relationship in such sales agreements is based on an approach in which it is expected that both sides will 'win' – will gain from the deal (albeit in different ways) – so that they start out with the intention of producing a mutually beneficial arrangement. At long last, an increasing number of organisations have come to see the relationship as one of interdependence, sometimes described as 'relationship management'. Here there is once more a managing of the investment in the customer, but in this case the investment is in the *direct* relationship involved.

You should note that it is not the personal relationship between the salesperson and the buyer that is paramount, although that will make its own contribution, but the relationship between the supplier organisation and the buying organisation. If you rely on personal relationships, they can all too quickly follow a salesperson to a competitor!

Customer account management

Probably the most important activity in developing these key relationships is the development of a sound account plan. Unlike the overall sales plan, however, which will deal with groups of customers, each account plan (or 'key account plan') deals quite specifically with a single customer. If such a plan is produced internally within the selling organisation, it will be a productive exercise; if it is produced in co-operation with the customer, so that the resulting plan becomes a shared plan, it may make a major contribution to the development of that business relationship so that it becomes a genuine peer-to-peer relationship. Account management, in its most general sense covering prospects as well as customers, is the essence of professional salesmanship. Customer account management, in particular, is the epitome of this. It is probably the most important single skill (apart from selling itself) required of a sales professional; and yet, perhaps typically, it is almost entirely neglected by sales trainers.

Activity 5.7

Does your organisation use account management practices? How effectively does it use them?

➡ SALES CAMPAIGN METHODS

Over and above what I have described already in this chapter concerning the strategy and tractics of selling, certain other aspects of sales campaign methods need to be highlighted here.

Sales promotions

This used to be associated with 'closing' a sale, in particular with price reductions as a final incentive to place the order. This is the sort of approach you may have been on the receiving end of: '... For today only, I can offer you a special deal on price!' Such devices are now just as frequently used in mass marketing. They are, however, very different from the promotional techniques that have been described so far, in terms of investment, since sales promotions are essentially short-term activities that can for once be considered as an operating cost rather than an investment. They are normally used to stimulate some specific action in the short term, typically offering a powerful additional factor added to the competitive balance to sway current sales in the supplier's favour; and to bring forward sales, or occasionally to generate extra sales. The main benefit, therefore, must usually be the (short-term) increase in sales; and the great majority of sales promotions are designed to boost current sales (for a short period of time).

But sales promotions can also be targeted to achieve other objectives – to increase repeat purchases amongst existing customers, to recruit specific competitors' customers etc. Indeed, it is sometimes argued that even by offering 15% more product for the same price – a typical device, and one that is much cheaper for the supplier to provide than the seemingly equivalent 15% off the price – extra sales can be produced over the longer term through increasing usage; but that is a dubious claim, as are most in this field, and is backed up by hardly any evidence.

The key characteristic of sales promotions is that almost all their effect is immediate. There is rarely any lasting increase in sales, and many of the costs – not least the management/salesforce time and effort – are typically not accounted for in the reported direct costs. Worse, they can conflict with the main brand messages and confuse the customer as to what the image really is: is it the high-quality product shown in the adverts, or is it the cut-price product in the promotion? Indeed, perhaps the most obvious disadvantage, which applies to many types of promotion, is that a price-cut is being offered, and this persuades users to expect a lower price in future – as well as, at the same time, potentially damaging any element of 'quality' in the image.

The greatest practical disadvantage of special sales promotions, though, may be their lack of effectiveness: research has shown that for many, probably most, promotions, the cost of selling a pound's-worth of sales is greater than that one pound received; in other words, promotions often actually make a loss, even in the short term! As such, the regular use of sales promotions on a large scale must be questioned. As a general device for promoting brands, they are expensive, ineffective and often damaging. The short-term sales increases that undoubtedly result are usually brought at the expense of the long-term investment in the brand, and may eventually lead to its demise.

Just occasionally, promotions may be used very effectively to achieve certain limited objectives. In particular, some are used to induce trial purchase, the classic example being money-off coupons distributed house to house (or in the press), or even samples of a new product at the time of its launch.

The major difficulty is that, despite all the above facts, which are well known and well documented, despite the proven ineffectiveness of almost all sales promotions, despite the fact that less than one-tenth of markets are price-sensitive, in recent years they have come to take more than half of all promotional spending! There surely can be only one reason for this: they generate the sort of the short-term business demanded by companies for whom short-termism is the dominant strategy. The only saving grace of sales promotions is that, being obviously short-term, the price cutting that they represent may not lead to a long-term price war, which can be even more debilitating.

> Does your organisation use sales promotions, especially cut-price offers? How effective are they? Do you (or senior management) know whether they are cost-effective, or possibly even make a loss?

That is all I am going to say about sales promotions, which you may think is all that needs to be said. But remember just how much effort and money is wasted on them! My advice is simple: no matter what anyone else says, do not use sales promotions!

Direct marketing

Direct marketing is rather a strange animal, lying somewhere between the interaction available with face-to-face selling and the cost-effectiveness of mass-market advertising. Thus, it aims to have a type of individual relationship with the customer, but at a distance. Classically, it has been the world of direct mail; and it is indicative of the problems this has faced that it is popularly known as 'junk mail'! Even so, let us examine how it operates for, as we will see, it may become rather more important in the future. In the traditional form, you simply mail a tightly targeted group of people with the message you want to broadcast, or in the new terminology to 'narrowcast' (which implies a much more tightly defined audience), and then, maybe, you invite them to reply and start a (mail) dialogue.

The elements of this process, which also form the basis of the more recent development we will look at later, are as follows:

- **The list**. The first requirement is that you have a list of the people who are likely to form your target audience, the potential buyers for your product or service. To start with, you will probably have to buy other people's lists, and there are mailing houses that specialise in almost every sort of list, from CEOs of multinationals down to trainspotters. But, best of all, is your own list – painstakingly built up over the years – which incorporates all that you have learnt about your customers.

- **The letter**. You have something that advertisements cannot aspire to: a personal letter, the writing of which is a type of art form and which demands a great deal of the right sort of skill. Some experts swear by the short letter and some say that the long one is best (and a PS at the bottom best of all!). It also demands considerable effort in polishing its every word. Best of all it can be personalised, addressed to the individual; and simply putting their name on its increases the response rate by a factor of two or three. Then, ideally, the content should be (computer) written with their known needs in mind – but this rarely happens: just adding that you know the town they live in fools nobody.

- **The inserts**. It is likely that you will put in with the letter the range of advertising material you would like to use in any advertising campaign. The only advice here is to limit it to one or two items; stuffing the envelope full of material – as most companies do – merely confuses the recipient and almost guarantees it will end in the waste basket. The essence of direct mail is to find the greatest number of excuses to mail follow-up letters.

- **The reply-paid card**. Most of all, should you want to get a dialogue started; so you want them to communicate with you – at least with their name and address. Again, personalisation of the reply-paid card – so that they only have to put it in the post – wins a much higher response rate.

- **The dialogue**. The dividends come when you are able to continue a dialogue with the prospect about the range of products you have to offer. The CD and book clubs (and, of course, Reader's Digest), typically make the best and most sophisticated use of this aspect; but the mail-order houses – which depend entirely on this for their business – are the biggest (albeit unsophisticated) users.

There are lots of books written about direct mail, but beware the overenthusiasm of most of these. Use your common sense for, as in all aspects of popular marketing literature, just because their authors believe what they are saying doesn't mean it is true!

Activity 5.9

Try to get a sample of your organisation's mailshot material. How

effective is it for you, and how effective do you think it might be
with customers?

Database marketing

It has always been what you *do* with the information you gather,
previously through direct mail, that has been important. That is
why the CD and book clubs have been so successful: they have a
very clear idea of what they will use it for – and they use it again
and again. Now, though, two major developments have greatly
expanded the opportunities; and forcibly brought it to the
attention of mainstream marketers who have for too long dismissed direct mail as an inferior medium.

First, the massive increase in computing power during the 1990s
has meant that the technical ability to manipulate the data – held
on databases (hence 'database marketing') – is far increased, so that
the interaction with the consumer (so far, typically through mail)
can nowadays be really personalised to take account of all you
know about that consumer's needs. But this has still had relatively
little impact. The real growth in potential has come about,
secondly, because of the rapidly growing number of large databases. Some of these have come about because organisations (such
as the banks and the large chain-stores) have started to recognise
the value of their own customer details or have started to recruit
users to their own clubs. Most important of all, perhaps, the
supermarkets have started clubs. These may have, so far, simply
offered a promotional device to lock in customers (with a rather
feeble, but still effective, 1% discount). But the real gold is in the
data they are collecting – in 'data warehouses' – about the detailed
buying habits of their millions of club members.

The (major) problem turns out to be accessing ('mining') this
data in a meaningful way. It is easy enough to put data into the
warehouses, and it is easy enough to get data out on a single
individual and then (manually) use that data. But how do you do
this on the mass scale needed to make database marketing viable?
So far, apart from the traditional users of direct mail, the only well
known example has been Sears, which used the data it held on
buyers of electrical goods to sell equipment insurance to those
without warranties. But that is hardly a sophisticated example of

database marketing; and the fairly typical example of my 83-year-old mother who is continually sent invitations to join her bank's student loan scheme suggests that we still have a long way to go!

The supermarket owners are working hard on the problem, their pre-occupation with the world of higher mathematics (one source of ideas) came as something of a shock to me (when compared with the very mundane problems the previous generations of their managers faced). So, eventually, a way of positively building on the individual relationships with their customers will be found and that massive potential will be tapped (not least, perhaps, so that their staff can call you by your own name as the corner-shop owners used to do in a more leisurely age). But they have some way to go yet!

Activity 5.10

Try to find out what active 'databases' of information your organisation holds about its customers. What use is made of them? How effective is this use? What more could be done? What 'databases' – in the broadest sense – does your own group hold? How well does it maintain, and use, them?

The Internet

The use of the Internet for selling has recently become a fashionable topic in marketing and it will eventually become genuinely important. However, it will not displace the rest of marketing until the next century, and in any case it follows most of the existing rules of marketing and almost all of those of direct mail. It just allows the 'mail' to be much more efficient and much more interactive. The problems will be for the advertising executives – those who have previously dismissed direct mail as worthless and who will now need to learn a whole set of new tricks!

➡ CUSTOMER SATISFACTION

I will finish this chapter on selling by looking at perhaps the most important element of relationship management in general, and that is customer satisfaction. Clearly, if it was not already obvious, any organisation should be highly motivated to make certain that its customers are satisfied. Yet, in practice, remarkably few do so! Thus, as a first step, it is essential that an organisation monitors the satisfaction level of its customers. This may be, all else failing, at the global level; as measured by market research. Preferably, though, it should be at the level of the individuals or groups.

IBM, at the peak of its success, every year conducted a survey of all its direct customers. The results were not just analysed to produce overall satisfaction indices, though that was done (and senior management viewed any deterioration with alarm), but they were also provided to field management so that they could rectify any individual problem situations.

There are a number of important advantages arising from the use of satisfaction surveys (particularly where any individual problems highlighted can be subsequently dealt with):

- Like complaints, satisfaction surveys indicate where problems are emerging, for rectification before they threaten the organisation's reputation.

- If the surveys cover all customers, they allow the 96% of people who simply do not complain (but may still feel aggrieved about their problems) to communicate their feelings and observations.

- Such surveys positively show, even to satisfied customers, that their supplier is interested in them.

- They help persuade the supplier's staff to take customer service more seriously.

In contrast, the aspect of customer or client service recognised by most organisations is simply that of customer *service levels*: the product should be available when and where the customer wants it, or a sale may be lost. There is a very clear trade-off here between customer service (level) and cost – although, fortunately, it seems that customers are not significantly affected by minor variations in service if there are generally high levels of product availability.

But customer satisfaction is often much more complex than you might expect. Thus, its effective level can be expressed by the surprising formula: *satisfaction equals perception minus expectation*, which takes into account what you feel it *should* be. Thus, if you expect a certain level of service and perceive the service received to be higher, you will be a satisfied customer. If you perceive this same level where you had expected a higher one, you will be disappointed and therefore a dissatisfied customer. The important point is that both what is perceived and what is expected are psychological phenomena, not reality; and it is the *relative* level of service – relative to expectations – that is important, not the absolute level. So give good service, but above all do not promise more than you can deliver! This is a lesson which too few marketers recognise, but which – perhaps fortunately for them – their cynical customers have learned well; they already discount much of the hype in advertising!

Activity 5.11

How does your organisation monitor customer satisfaction? How seriously does it take any results?

How satisfied are your organisation's customers? How satisfied are those of your own group?

Inner marketing

This is a suitable time to talk about one unusual aspect of our subject. Marketing is, by definition, primarily concerned with the world outside the organisation. On the other hand, if it is to maximise customer satisfaction and at the same time optimise the use of the resources, it also has to be concerned with what lies *inside* the organisational perimeter. This is 'inner marketing'.

Increasingly, the most valuable resource of any organisation (and particularly those in the service sector) is its people, together with the skills they possess. In tapping this internal resource, so that the organisation can face up to its external environment, it turns out that many of the traditional tools of marketing can be used to great effect in the very important areas of internal communication and motivation, of harnessing and focusing this (people) resource to meet the objectives of the marketing plan.

Recently, such campaigns have tended to focus on Total Quality Management (TQM) on the basis that the overall quality perceived by the customer comes from every part of the organisation – from support and administration staff just as much as from the workers (or the robots) on the production lines. Inner marketing is in many ways, therefore, the ulitmate extension of TQM in that it fixes 'quality' exclusively in terms of the marketing context (of what is important to the customer) for every employee.

Inner marketing is a powerful concept. It says quite simply that employees should be marketed to in exactly the same way as customers; after all, it is now widely recognised that both groups are key 'stakeholders'. Implicit in this concept (which should not be confused with the internal market) is that all the aspects of marketing as a whole should be incorporated – in particular, that a dialogue should take place between employees and employers (via the marketers sometimes). Inner marketing is as much about finding out what the employees want as persuading them to do what the organisation wants! Such internal research may have great benefits; 'opinion surveys' are remarkably effective devices for obtaining information on the inner market. If applied regularly to all staff, such surveys are also remarkably good motivators and contributors to a positive culture.

The first requirement, and the one that distinguishes it from almost all other (internal and external) customer service programmes, is some form of marketing research – exactly as with any other marketing programme, but here conducted on the organisation's own employees. This should be used to determine where the employees stand, for example, in relation to their perception of the customer (Is the customer seen as friend or foe?) – and of the customer service programmes that are likely to be the main focus of the research (Does anyone do anything more than pay lip-service to them? Why?). Moreover, as with any piece of sound research, it should also attempt to find out where employees might wish to stand in the future, exploring their attitudes and motivations (Do you really want to offer a good service? If not, why not? How can you be persuaded to change your views?). The outcome of this is most productively described as 'consensus', since this best incorporates the attitude of mind that should lie behind it: the search should be positively designed to find the outcomes, especially in terms of values, to which all the participants (in this context, members of staff at all levels, but also the managers and customers who will also have to accept these) will be able to commit themselves.

Only with this basic information on employee attitudes (however derived) can the 'inner marketer' start to devise the programmes necessary to create the new attitudes, the conviction in the goals handed down to them, that will deliver the requisite service to the external customers. The actions needed to achieve the end results follow the well trodden path of any marketing campaign, although they are alien to much of human resource management. At the most basic level, the staff will need to understand what is expected of them – by their own management and, in particular, by their customers. It is remarkable how many 'improvements' in customer service are advertised to the customers but never explained to the employees who are to deliver them, let alone agreed with those employees.

Activity 5.12

How does your organisation treat you? (This is probably one answer that will come easily, and you will likely have discussed it many times with your colleagues and (hopefully) in your personal appraisal reviews.)

How satisfied are you, and how does this affect your attitude to your work? What does the organisation need to do to better earn your loyalty?

What do you need to do to earn the loyalty of your own group?

Chapter 6
Mass advertising

We now move on to the opposite end of the spectrum, to the forms of marketing that deal with mass audiences where the ideal of simple face-to-face communication cannot be applied. The reasons are usually economic, where this form of communication simply cannot be afforded, but it would also be impractical in many of the markets in which it is used – we have already discussed the problems emerging in database marketing as a result of trying to handle large numbers of customers on an individual basis.

Having said all of that, many of the *principles* of face-to-face selling still apply to mass marketing. Indeed, sitting at home in front of your television bombarded by product commercials created by marketers, it may seem a strange concept to grasp but the idea of the dialogue applies just as powerfully to mass advertising. What is very different is the way that this dialogue is conducted.

We have already seen how a dialogue starts: the 'listening' element provided by market research, continued into the 'talking' part of the dialogue. At that stage, you need to check how well the messages you have created, and the media you are using to transmit them, are performing, in order to make certain that your campaign is actually working. Once more, I should reiterate that mass advertising is just one part of the overall promotional mix. Your campaign will probably contain a number of different elements, but here – as the pre-eminent mass medium – advertising is likely to dominate the other elements.

In setting up your campaign, it is the decisions that should have already been made, and that refer to the overall shape of the marketing mix, that count. In particular, the product positioning should define what your advertising needs to achieve. The advertising message should emerge naturally from what you wish to say about your product, and the media will be defined by the target audience(s) you have selected. You will now understand why I stressed so strongly the lessons of positioning. But all of this will come as nasty surprise for many advertising people, especially the creative and media teams in agencies, who will still try to convince you that the choice of message and media starts with their own deliberations! You must ignore their seductive voices, and insist on advertising that does the job demanded of it and that continues the dialogue you have started with potential customers. This is not to say that you should be too rigid in your views; I have many times relaxed the positioning requirements to allow creative campaigns that brilliantly conveyed something close to the message I wanted; but I have never totally abandoned my core positioning requirement, no matter how tearfully the creative teams pleaded.

Activity 6.1

In your opinion, to what extent does your organisation's advertising message naturally follow from the 'product package', or does it reflect (advertising agency) creative decisions? What should it do?

➡ INVESTMENT IN ADVERTISING

At this stage it is worthwhile bringing into the open another popular misconception, which is held especially strongly by agencies, and that is that each advertising campaign – indeed each advert – stands alone. This is an understandable wish, again by agency creative departments who want to have a free hand (the artist, still alive in many of them, facing the challenge of a blank canvas), but unfortunately it is not supported by customers, who are only too well aware of what has gone before. Unless it is a totally new product, the campaign will have to allow for the product's historical activities. But, first of all, let's look at the impact of advertising in general.

The comments that I am about to make about the longer-term impacts of advertising also apply to *all* other forms of marketing promotion (including selling). The notable exception is sales promotions, which, as we have see, are determinedly short-term in ambitions. All the evidence supports the notion that every other promotional activity, advertising in particular, will have an impact over an extended period of time. Indeed, the evidence suggests that the 'sales' impact of most advertising campaigns peaks several months after the campaign is run and (good news for those following the philosophy of the Competitive Saw) will then last for some months – perhaps even a year or more. But, whatever the timescale (and it obviously varies from product to product), investment in advertising almost never has an immediate impact on overall sales. Furthermore, this investment is cumulative: advertising *now* builds on that which has gone before it in the past. It is that cumulative level that really counts towards producing sales.

Returning to the Competitive Saw, which we looked at in Chapter 4, I simplified matters there somewhat when I suggested that performance – specifically in terms of market share – increases immediately. It may be, and indeed should be, that *awareness* of a product or brand rises immediately after the stimulus (an advertising burst, say), and that is the performance by which you should judge your success. But overall sales growth will usually lag, and this is one reason why researchers find it so hard to measure the sales productivity of advertising.

In most cases, for mature brands, the competitive saw looks much like the basic version that we have talked about earlier (see Figure 4.3): a series of fluctuations around a level average. In other words, there may be temporary ups and downs in the fortunes of the brand, but over time these will even out. The exceptions to this rule are, however, important, especially in the context of advertising or other promotional investment.

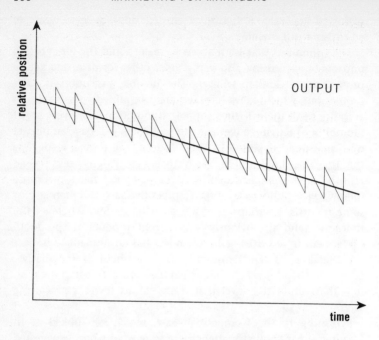

Figure 6.1: The Competitive Saw with a declining trend

As you can see from the example in Figure 6.1, the fluctuations can hide a declining trend over the longer term. What is being done in the shorter term is simply not sufficient to keep the brand alive; it really is in terminal decline. This may be because, over time, there is a slow drift away from the ideal position as the customers' needs and wants change and/or competitive positioning improves. Such a slow drift is easy to miss for, as we have seen, the lag in advertising impact is difficult to track. Thus, many organisations simply do not realise it is happening; they save money in the short term and unknowingly mortgage their position in the longer term.

Your response to this situation may take two forms. The first, and perhaps the most effective, is that of dynamic repositioning. The change in relative positions should be regularly tracked and the brand's position readjusted to take account of this, exactly as the basic Competitive Saw diagram suggests. If such dynamic repositioning is not possible, perhaps because the necessary product changes come in discrete steps, then occasional more significant readjustments may be needed (see Figure 6.2). This is where the concept of 'advertising depreciation' allows the build-up of reserves to cover the significant costs of such major repositioning exercises. In the opposite direction, if you increase your ongoing investment levels in the spend on each advertising burst or on their frequency, you should be able to improve your long-term position. This does, however, depend upon what others are doing at the same time; so the concept of 'share of advertising', namely your relative advertising level (against competitors), may be more important than its absolute level.

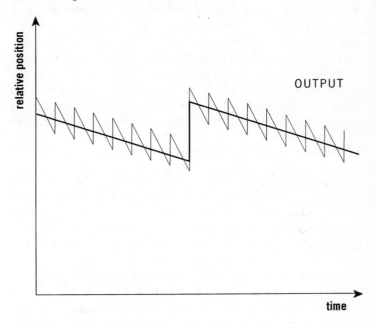

Figure 6.2: The Competitive Saw with recovery from decline

The second aspect of advertising over time is that, except for a totally new product where there really is a clean slate, any advertising campaign must always be linked – in the customer's mind, at least – to what went before. I suspect that, when you think about your favourite brands, you probably think about them in terms of the advertising campaign that caught your imagination, no matter how long ago. How many of us remember Coca-Cola's 'I want to teach the world to sing' campaign? Again, this is a fact that many agencies, or at least their creative teams, can't seem to grasp. They are too prone to assume they have a blank slate on which to show their creative genius. At a more mundane level, most of the marketing people who commission and create advertisements become bored with them far too quickly. They forget that they have been examining them day after day, in rough and proof form, for months before the customer sees them. As a result, far too many effective campaigns bite the dust before they have proved their worth. On the other hand, the most successful advertising campaign I ever instituted ran for the best part of a quarter of a century almost unchanged!

In this way, often the most important (and certainly the most neglected) aspect of any new campaign should be how well it builds on the previous ones. Unfortunately, in practice they are too often contradictory; which means that the new campaign doesn't just have to build the brand's position but also has to fight its way through the legacy of the old campaign(s) before it can even start! So you must be aware of the advertising history – which in the old days of press advertisement was lovingly preserved in the aptly named 'guard books' ('family albums' of carefully preserved advertisements).

Activity 6.2

Can you roughly trace the impact of your organisation's advertising over time? How well have the various advertising campaigns built on each other? Were any of them contradictory?

➡ THE MESSAGE

As we have seen, the offer you will be able to make in all your promotional campaigns, not just in your advertising, should have already been defined by the work we have looked at in the earlier chapters of this book. The promotional message is inherent in the 'marketing mix' you have specified. And I cannot overstress just how important it is to start with some form of positioning exercise as the framework for your advertising; otherwise, you may be at the mercy of the agency's creative department! In this context, the message is not added as free-standing ornamentation by the advertising agency; it is, instead, an integral part of the package. To try to add anything to it would not merely be to gild the lily but to reduce the impact of the main message. Indeed, what best meets the needs and wants of the customer, the product offer, should be the most powerful message you can convey to the customer. All that remains thereafter is to deliver that message to the customer.

At the other extreme, the message must not offer more than you can in reality deliver. We have seen that *satisfaction equals perception minus expectation*. If you raise the customer's expectations too high, his or her perceptions of the actual performance will almost certainly fall short of these, resulting in disappointment. On the other hand, if you don't raise expectations high enough, you may not make the sale in the first place – hence the need to achieve exactly the right balance.

After a nailing down of what it is that you actually offer, however, the secret of great promotion is then to communicate that as brilliantly and powerfully as you can. That is where, at long last, the all important creative element should enter, and this is where the real creativity in the advertising agency should pay dividends. Unfortunately, in terms of the advice I can offer, apart from rather mundane descriptions of the communication process described earlier, there is remarkably little suitable theory around to help you with this. Practice is dominated by creative solutions. This is inevitably where the task is to make your offering stand out from the many others that confront the customer, to make even detergents seem interesting and important. But at least you can then test how impactful it is, and how well it conveys your chosen message, by using market research to test it. Before we move on, however, let me reiterate that no matter how creative the final message is, it *must* match the needs of the product/service package.

There is, though, a progression of the various types of advertising copy. We can start, say, with the (press advertisement) headline, which necessarily has to be short and impactful since it has to grab your attention as you leaf through the newspaper;

then, as the next step up, there is the 'body copy', the longer selling message that is built into the smaller typeface in the rest of the ad, and this has to get you interested in the 'product' and start to change your attitudes so that you will be persuaded to buy (a monumental task in a few dozen words, which is why good copywriters are worth so much); then come the brochures, which spell out the message in even more detail; and the pack itself, at the point of sale, which must also demand your attention and, in its own body copy, continue the selling process; and, finally, there are the instructions on the leaflet inside the pack, which are almost invariably forgotten as a sales message but which can convert the purchaser into a loyal recommender to friends. This takes us back to the often overlooked point that advertising has to develop peer group influences as much as make a direct impact on potential customers: so much advertising needs (primarily) to reinforce the attitudes of existing users.

At all of these levels, perhaps the best advice of all is KISS (Keep It Simple Stupid). This is another way of saying 'less is more', a philosophy that is especially relevant in the case of advertising and other forms of promotion: the simpler the message, the greater the impact it will make and the greater the attention it will receive.

Activity 6.3

How effectively are the various levels of 'copy' used by your own organisation? How well do they support existing users?

➡ THE IDEAL MEDIUM FOR THE MESSAGE

Let us now look at the vehicle, the medium, that will be chosen to carry the message. In the wider context, this can extend from the face-to-face selling that we looked at in the previous chapter, through to the advertising that we are examining here. In practice, as we have seen, it will be a mix – the promotional mix – of a number of these elements. When we come to the specific choice(s), though, the single most important factor is frequently the size of the budget – although most theory would hold otherwise. At one extreme, if you have a small budget, you may be restricted to appearing in a range of very specialist media (possibly just in the small ads); at the other, with a multimillion-dollar budget, only television may be big enough to absorb such an investment.

Even then, most advertising is in practice concentrated into bursts, where it achieves the higher impact needed to overcome the potential customers' inertia, rather than being shown continuously (see Figure 6.3). Indeed, even the heaviest advertisers use this approach, since the impact is not just determined by the absolute levels of expenditure but also by the levels relative to competitors.

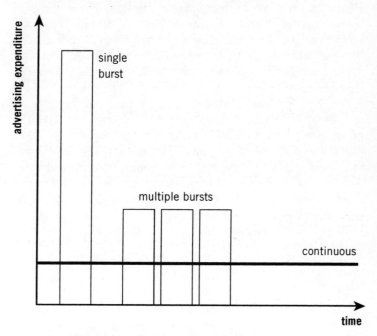

Figure 6.3: Different advertising campaign profiles

Within the limitations set by the budget, there are two dimensions by which the pattern of delivery is judged. The most basic of these dimensions is coverage, for the cost of reaching the last few per cent of the population grows exponentially. It is convenient to think of it as a variant of the 80:20 Rule, although in this case quite simply the 80% Rule: anything over 80% coverage of any market or segment rapidly becomes prohibitively expensive. At the other extreme, the requirement for coverage of very specialised segments is precision. There is simply no justification for coverage of those not in the target segment, although specialist markets will be much more difficult to reach without such wastage.

The other dimension is that of the degree of the individual's exposure to the campaign. It is not sufficient to provide the customer with just one opportunity to see your advertisement; indeed, it is generally agreed that customers need to see any advertisement a number of times before it has any significant effect. The usual rule of thumb is that five OTSs (opportunities to see) are needed to achieve adequate impact. This may mean that you will need to 'air' your commercial, say, up to 20 or 30 times – far more than most people would imagine – and this explains why, if you are unlucky, you always seem to be seeing the commercial you hate most!

The skill of the advertising agency's media planners is in balancing these contradictory requirements. However, it should be noted that by the time your agency's media buyers have taken advantage of all the special offers put out by the media owners, your final schedules may look very different from those decided purely on such targeting. So, once more, the answer is that you must be pragmatic and leave this to the experts; just as long as you are sure you really have the best experts in your team! Your own contribution is in choosing the right advertising agency, and then working with them.

Media options

To build the desired exposure patterns, a *mix* of specific media is often used. Which ones you use will depend upon the specific audience you need to reach, but the broad performance of the main types, against some key dimensions, is shown in Figure 6.4.

In terms of overall advertising expenditures, media advertising is dominated by the press and television, which are of comparable size by value of sales. Posters and radio follow some way behind, with cinema now representing a very specialist medium. Spending in the press is dominated by the national and regional newspapers, with the latter taking almost all of the classified advertising revenue.

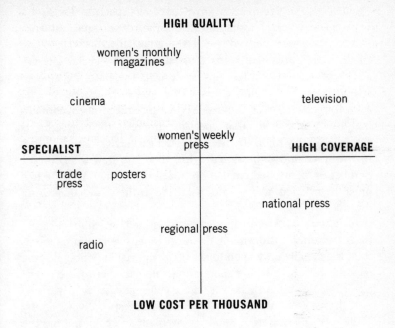

Figure 6.4: The spread of media types in advertising

National newspapers are obviously best matched to national advertisers that are happy with black-and-white as well as some colour advertisements. These newspapers are supposed to carry more 'weight' (i.e. authority) with their readers since they are deliberately read, not treated just as 'background'. Regional newspapers may be dailies, which look and perform much like the nationals, or weeklies, but are rather more specialised and are often supposed to carry less 'weight' because they dominate the market for classified advertising. Indeed, there is usually much more advertising competing for the readers' attention, and the weekly newspapers are fast becoming the province of the free newspapers that are typically delivered without change to all homes in a given area. They obtain all their revenue from the very high proportion of advertising that they carry, and accordingly having the least 'weight' of all.

The magazines and trade/technical journal market sector are

about the same size as each other, but less than half that of the newspaper sector. Magazines offer a more selective audience (which is more 'involved', with the editorial at least) and are traditionally categorised into 'general interest', 'special interest' and 'trade/technical'. The advertiser will, therefore, be able to select those that match the specific profile demanded by the advertising strategy. The audience is usually concentrated, containing only those with that specialist interest; their 'weight' is correspondingly high; and they can offer excellent colour facilities. In the trade and professional fields, there are now a significant number of 'controlled circulation' magazines; which like the free press mentioned above, are paid for entirely by advertising revenue.

Television is the most important mass medium, albeit a rather transitory one. It is normally the most expensive medium, and as such is generally only open to the major advertisers (though some regional contractors offer more affordable packages to their local advertisers). It offers by far the widest coverage, particularly in the peak hours (roughly 7.00–10.30 p.m.), and especially to family audiences. Offering sight, sound, movement and colour, it has the greatest impact, especially for those products or services where a 'demonstration' is essential since it combines the virtues of both the storyteller and the demonstrator. To be effective, however, these messages must be kept simple and yet have the impact to overcome the surrounding distractions of family life. The price structures can be horrendously complicated, with the 'rate card' (the price list) offering different prices for different times throughout the day; and this is further complicated by a wide range of special promotional packages and individual negotiations! It is truly the province of the expert media-buyer.

Posters represent something of a specialist medium, which is generally used in support of campaigns using other media. The use of radio has increased greatly in recent years, with the granting of many more licences. Radio typically generates specific audiences at different times of the day – for example, adults at breakfast, housewives thereafter, motorists in the rush hours – and it can be a very cost-effective way of reaching these groups. Although the numbers in the national cinema audience are now small, this may be the most effective medium for extending coverage to the younger age groups since the core audience is aged 15–24.

Activity 6.4

What media mix does your organisation use? Why? Does it get the coverage it needs, with sufficient 'opportunities to see' (OTS)?

➡ PUBLIC RELATIONS

One of the most powerful forms of promotion, the most efficient but often the most neglected, is that of 'PR'. This is variously said to stand for Public Relations, which may include a wide range of activities, or Press Relations, which concentrates on the more direct promotional aspect of paralleling advertising – placing stories in the editorial matter rather than the advertising space. Whichever is chosen as the definition, and I prefer to think of it simply as PR, it can be a very effective (and certainly the most cost-effective) part of the any marketing mix. My recommendation would be that PR should always be *first* on your list of budget priorities. In the narrower context of Press Relations, it is often a particularly valuable promotional device for services; since the 'authority' offered by independent recommendation in editorial matter can add vital credibility to an intangible service. It can, similarly, be especially important in building credibility for a new product.

There are a wide range of vehicles available for press relations, but the most important task of the PR professional is to maintain contact with the key journalists in the media (usually national press, journals, radio and television). It is not just sending out packages of pretty pictures, or inviting journalists to a free lunch, as many organisations seem to think it is: in reality, it is a sophisticated two way process, which needs to be the province of experts (often from an outside agency). The PR professional learns about, and can contribute to, features that will be appearing in the media; while, in the other direction, the journalists become more receptive to news stories from that PR professional. It is, once more, an *investment* process. You can't start with a clean slate and immediately get good editorial coverage, as too many marketing people expect. The relationship with the media (and especially with an individual journalist) has to be cultivated – over months and even years – until a mutual trust has been earned. When this is working properly, it is not a process of exploitation – by either side – but of mutual respect.

The backbone of PR is the news item, either genuine or 'manufactured', which shows the client product or service in a good light (and, most important, is interesting and entertaining enough to be run by the news media). Such stories are best placed, as described above, by personal contact. The most important aspect of any story, though, is that it should be newsworthy. In general, you get the PR coverage the story is worth. Consequently you need the professional (journalistic) experience to recognise just what is a newsworthy story (which may not be what the amateur would expect), and then to be able to present it in a way that interests a (very cynical) press corps. On the other hand, you need your own most senior managers (who have been *very* carefully briefed!) to front the story – the press are much more impressed by them than by PR departments. But it is like any other form of marketing: you must know the customers (here the journalists) and provide (and sell) the right 'product' (the story they want).

It is just as important that you are able to react to press enquiries. Investing in a continuously manned press office, which can immediately handle any level of question from journalists and is effusively enthusiastic to help, is essential if PR is to be taken seriously. Again, professionalism is required. Not least is the ability to find answers very quickly and to meet the urgent deadlines by which almost all journalists are driven – you can't ask them to 'hold the front page'. This is not an easy task, with journalists thinking in terms of hours, and sometimes of minutes, but your own managers – outside the press office – thinking in terms of days or even weeks. Time really is of the essence in this work.

Press Relations is very cost-effective, and the amount that can be spent on it is relatively low in comparison with the other promotional spends. Furthermore, expenditure is self-limiting – there are just so many events you can arrange, and just so many journalists you can entertain. Thus, there is a good argument for saying that, in setting budgets, PR should come at the head of the queue.

As a footnote, it is worth mentioning that many organisations leave the PR to their trade associations. This is *wrong*. These bodies are often not as well respected by the media as they claim (they are, rightly sometimes, seen as lapdogs) and their agenda may not be the same as your own organisation's (they are often captured by pressure groups within the industry).

Activity 6.5

How does your organisation manage its press relations? How effective is it in obtaining valuable editorial coverage?

➡ CORPORATE RELATIONS

As mentioned in the previous section, PR is often used as a global term to cover a wider range of activities than just 'Press Relations'. Of this range, perhaps the most important may be that of acting as the formal corporate interface with the outside world. This aspect of PR is much more likely to be the province of internal corporate PR personnel rather than an external agency.

The organisation may find itself exposed to the activities of external pressure groups and the corporate PR department, if one exists, will typically be the one that defends the organisation against these onslaughts and handles the external interface with such groups. Rather fewer organisations use PR positively to influence external activities, such as those in the political arena, to their advantage. However, such action can prove very effective for those organisations which can afford it – and which can recruit the lobbyists who run such campaigns.

The first task of such a corporate PR department is to determine what 'issues', relevant to the future (survival) of the organisation, are likely to emerge over the next few years. As in 'scanning' the environment (which we will look at in Chapter 8), this is not an easy task. It can be directly based upon opinion research – though this may be expensive – or it can be obtained by buying syndicated reports from the specialist consultancies. Such research is important, however, in that it is much more effective to 'nip a problem in the bud' before it develops into something more troublesome.

Once the issues have 'emerged', or at least have been detected, it is important to try and understand them; and, in particular, to obtain political input on their perceived importance. It is also important to start 'lobbying' (possibly on an international scale) as soon as possible.

Activity 6.6

How does your organisation organise its formal (corporate) interface with outside groups? How effectively does it do this?

➡ DISTRIBUTION CHANNELS

I said I would eventually come to the fourth P of 'Place', and so I suppose I had better deliver on my promise by providing some coverage, albeit briefly. You will remember that this is the catch-all element of the four Ps. Its importance is most clearly justified, however, in the field of retailing. Here the famous saying used to be 'What you need is location, location, location': if your shop was literally on the wrong side of the high street, it could cut your sales by half. Now, with out-of-town developments dominating much of retailing, the elements of this are different; and with remote trading rapidly increasing (by telephone or, increasingly, via the Internet) this saying has lost a lot of its validity. Accessibility is now the key. No longer is your telephone directory operator located at your neighbourhood telephone exchange; he or she is much more likely to be found on a remote Scottish island (or, increasingly, in India, where labour costs are much lower)!

More widely, one special category of customers, namely those who control the distribution channels (be they retailers, wholesalers or agents), have requirements that are likely to be quite simple but very different from those of other customers. Their aims are the maximisation of profit and the minimisation of risk from the business arising from your own organisation. These 'customers' are also special, however, in that they also become, in effect, members of your salesforce.

'Place' is often also extended to cover the whole logistics of distribution, from inventory control of warehouse stocks to scheduling your transport – and for some products (such as fresh food being brought from the other side of the world) the advent of the 747 cargo airliners has revolutionised marketing. But, you will no doubt be glad to hear, this is beyond the scope of this book!

Activity 6.7

What distribution channels, if any, does your organisation use? How productive are they? What 'channels' does your own group use?

➡ CONVICTION MARKETING

So far we have assumed that there is just one category of marketing, albeit that it takes many forms. On the other hand, 'conviction marketing', which followed almost none of the basic rules of traditional marketing, is probably used more widely than pure marketing and often is just as successful. Indeed, the majority of the few truly global brands have embodied it to some degree: IBM, with its philosophy of 'customer service'; Coca-Cola, with its embodiment of the American teenage dream; and Marlboro, and the wide-open spaces of the frontier.

Unlike 'selling', which is conventionally seen as the main alternative to marketing, conviction marketing is very firmly centred on the consumer, as all marketing is supposed to be, but its focus is still one-sided. There is little attempt to find out what the consumers' needs or wants are. Instead, it is based on the powerful idea (the 'conviction'), to which the organisation believes the consumers also are (or should be) committed. Its essence is the power it gives to the marketing organisation to 'evangelise'. This power derives from a number of factors, given in the next paragraph.

The concept must be *distinctive*. Beyond that, it has to be *based on a strong brand personality*, which adds the necessary richness. It also has to be instantly *communicable*, which demands that it be clear; and preferably simple. It is, above all, *dependent upon the consumers' belief* in what its communicators say. So, under conviction marketing, the 'vision' of the product has to be conveyed convincingly to the target audience. Although customer needs are at the heart of conventional marketing, they are only an enabling factor in the case of conviction marketing. If the 'vision' is too far removed from the consumer's view of reality, it will not be accepted.

At the end of the day, the basic justification for conventional marketing, in the absence of the vision of the conviction marketer, is simply that – for most of us – it is still the most successful approach to product or service management. Giving the customer what he or she wants rarely fails!

➡ COARSE MARKETING

Real-life marketing needs to handle a limited number of factors based on imperfect information and using limited resources. Thus, for example, new products will emerge from irrational processes, and the rational development process may be used (if it is used at all) purely to screen out the worst non-runners. The design of the advertising and the packaging will be the output of the creative minds employed, which management will screen, often by 'gut reaction', to ensure that it is reasonable. Indeed, the most successful marketer is often the one who trains his or her 'gut reaction' to simulate that of the average customer! This almost instinctive management is what I would call 'coarse marketing'; to distinguish it from the refined and aesthetically pleasing form favoured by the theorists. Coarse-marketing matches the real-life world of most marketing!

Activity 6.8

How, in this context, would you characterise your organisation's approach to marketing: traditional, conviction or coarse?

How about the approach used by you and your group?

➡ INTERNATIONAL MARKETING

One aspect of marketing that preoccupies many books is that of the international dimension. In reality, depending upon the form of your organisation, the important fact to note is that even this typically followed the same rules as those that I have described in the rest of this book.

There are various definitions of the various types of organisations offered by different commentators, but the main types of structure, in terms of handling international business, are as follows:

- **Transnationals**. These are the organisations, such as IBM or Shell Oil, that operate in most countries, with marketing organisations in all of these and production units (and even development laboratories) in a fair number. These organisations can afford to view national markets as purely regional affairs, with each region having its own marketing characteristics but otherwise no special marketing problems.

- **Multinationals**. These organisations, such as Unilever and General Mills, also operate in many countries. However, they tend to have individual operating companies in each country, which market to (and manufacture for) just that market. Country organisations are, therefore, subsidiaries of the international organisation and they control their own country operations largely independently of the other country organisations. The marketing process is, thus, almost a purely national operation; with the parent company only controlling the operations at the group level (and then typically only in terms of the flow of funds).

- **International traders**. These are organisations, such as Renault and Nestlé that are typically based in one country and produce most of their output there. In other countries, they have sales subsidiaries. They are largely in the business of export. On the other hand, they already have the international structure which compartmentalises them – so that they too may be largely seen to be part of normal marketing activities.

- **Exporters**. These represent the majority of those organisations trading internationally, although only for a small part of their volume of trade. Their main base, often overwhelmingly so, is their 'domestic' (home) market. For them, exporting really is a very different activity.

- **Domestic producers**. It should not be forgotten that these companies form the largest number of organisations in any national market. They do not in any way involve themselves in overseas markets – perhaps wisely so, where many small export operations are loss-makers.

Standardisation versus adaptation

For almost all these various types of organisation, therefore, there is nothing special about international marketing and it is business as usual. Indeed, for those who operate in this way across national boundaries, there is just one extra question, with two possible answers: should we choose 'standardisation' (that is, the standardisation of products across all markets) or 'adaptation' (the classic marketing approach to the individual needs of markets/consumers separately in each national market). Thereafter, they can get on with marketing as usual!

Export or not?

For the organisations that do see international marketing as something rather different – the exporters – in general there are three main initial decisions for their international marketing operations:

- Do we undertake international marketing operations at all?
- If 'yes', then in what individual country markets?
- And by what means?

The first question to be asked, therefore, of organisations that are currently limited to their national market, is quite simply whether they should export at all. There is often a considerable amount of 'emotional' pressure on medium-sized firms, not least from governments that want to improve their sagging balances of trade, to 'export'. The reality is that, apart from the ubiquitous multinationals, probably very few organisations benefit significantly, at least in financial terms, from their 'international operations'.

If the answer to that first question is 'yes', then the organisation needs to get expert help in answering the other two! There are many specialist books written on the subject, and Michael Czinkotta, the co-author of my own US textbook, has written one of the best-selling of them. However, since you can lose large amounts of money on such ventures, please do get the best possible (independent) advice.

Activity 6.9

How does your organisation handle international operations? Does it 'standardise' or 'adapt'? How different, in practice, is its international marketing to its equivalent domestic (home market) operations?

Chapter 7
Planning for success

The climax of most marketing books, especially textbooks, is the chapter on strategy. This is where the lessons are supposed to come together; this is where you carefully craft the plans that will lead to your ultimate success. This is also the chapter, typically at the end of the book, where even more myths are perpetuated. It is, for example, where the Boston Matrix and the Product Life Cycle, both of which we have already looked at (and dismissed) in Chapter 4, are introduced. Success, according to these myths, can be guaranteed by following a few simple laws.

I hope that, by now, you realise that this is definitely *not* my own view of successful marketing. Indeed, marketing success comes about by a combination, a *unique* combination for each organisation, of all the things we talked about. There is no single easy route to success. This chapter on 'strategy' is, therefore, about how you should bring all these elements together in the combination that is most effective for your own highly individual organisation. We shall also, at the end of this chapter and in the next, look at how these ideas can be extended into the wider environment.

➡ MARKETING PLANNING

Having put forward all of these caveats, I still believe that the marketing planning exercise – which most organisations feel obliged to undertake once a year – is valuable, not least because it is the *only* time most organisations think rationally about the subject! So, let's have a look at what it entails in its simplest possible form.

Reduced to its basics, it comprises three simple questions:

- Where are you now?
- Where to you want to be?
- How do you get there?

We examine each of these three questions below.

Where are you now?

This is what the earlier part of the book was about, especially Chapters 2 and 3 about customers and the market research processes that let you explore their needs and wants. More specifically, the actual starting point – in the context of a marketing plan – must be a definitive statement, ideally a formal 'map' of some kind, of where you – as a result of your investigations – believe your product/service package(s) currently lies in terms of the market, and what are your core competences.

This recognition of where you are starting from is arguably the most important step of all, and the one where most organisations fail. If you cannot recognise where you *currently* are (in terms of what really matters, especially to your customers) then you will not be able to plot how you will reach your objectives. We have looked at these processes individually. The only differences, at the level of the marketing plans, is that you have to review them rather more carefully and, in particular, you must integrate them into one meaningful overall picture of where you currently are – which, with so many distractions to deal with (with so many trees which hide the wood) – is often easier said than done. It is too easy, and such good fun, to get immersed in the detail – which is another reason why the discipline imposed by the annual plan is so important.

Even then, it is essential to spell out the assumptions you are making. Most organisations do not even realise that they make assumptions. You should, however, make as few of them as possible; and very carefully explain those that you do make.

Ideally, as an extension to this process, when (in the later steps) you estimate the results expected from your strategies, you should also explore a range of alternative assumptions. It is also useful to incorporate positioning maps (see Figure 2.2) at this stage because many managers, like myself, find that such maps show us much more clearly where we are, where verbal descriptions are easily misinterpreted.

Activity 7.1

Where are you now? Briefly describe how you see the current position of your organisation's brands in marketing terms.

Where, similarly, is your own group?

Where do you want to be?

Perhaps the most important activity that is specific to the planning stages of marketing, is formally deciding where you want to be in the future. The organisation will already have existing marketing objectives, by design or by default, and these will severely limit your freedom of action. Whatever their origins, the marketing objectives may often contribute the most important elements of the overall corporate objectives – where the organisation primarily justifies its existence in terms of what it offers to its customers or clients. The marketing objectives must, in any case, complement these corporate objectives. The former typically relate to what products will be where in what markets, and must be realistically based on customer behaviour in those markets. They are essentially about the match between those products and the markets. Furthermore, these objectives must emerge naturally from the product/service package and the organisational core competences.

To be most effective, the marketing objectives should preferably be capable of measurement, and therefore be quantifiable. This measurement may be in terms of sales volume, sales (money) value, market share, percentage penetration of distribution outlets, and so on. One caveat, though: formal corporate objectives tend to be documented in terms of profit projections – our managerial culture demands as much – but the unpublished, informal objectives that really drive the actions of most organisations range much wider. It is these wider objectives that also need to be taken into account here. Even so, as far as possible, the relatively general long-term objectives need to be quantified as a series of targets – and given timescales as well as numerical projections. Even intangible objectives, such as those relating to image, should be quantified in terms of measurable marketing research results. Ideally, some space should be dedicated to (two dimensional) maps of the most important parameters, showing on each the current position (along with that of the customers' ideal choice and that of key competitors' actuals), the targeted future positions and the planned path to these. This should, again ideally, be used to summarise the whole plan, but should in the process also be used as a further check on the validity of the proposed moves.

A problem that can arise is that the objectives may be much more complex than the existing processes, with their emphasis on simple 'wish-fulfilment', will allow for. But they must be achieveable; otherwise, in publishing them, you are simply going to demoralise your staff. If nothing else, the objectives have to allow for reality; they have to take into account your limitations as much as your potentials. Conversely, they should not be undemanding; they must push the organisation towards developing its full potential.

Activity 7.2

What are your organisation's marketing objectives? Are they realistic, achievable? Do they take into account what is really important, and do they stretch the organisation to near its full potential?

What are your group's objectives? Are they realistic, and yet stretch your capabilities to the full?

Corporate mission

In recent years it has become very fashionable to describe a 'corporate mission', which provides the context for the corporate objectives, and most organisations now routinely include such a statement as part of their annual report. This 'corporate mission' can be thought of as a definition of what the organisation is, of what it does: 'Our business is....' Unfortunately, as with most fashions in management theory, it has now become an almost meaningless appendage. To be effective, it must have real teeth. Indeed, perhaps the most important factor in successful marketing is a genuine 'corporate vision' rather than a bland 'mission'. Surprisingly, in view of its wider importance, this aspect of 'vision' planning is one that is often neglected by marketing textbooks – though not by the popular exponents of corporate strategy.

If the organisation in general, and its chief executive in particular, has a strong vision of where its future lies, then there is a good chance that the organisation will achieve a strong position in its markets (and attain that future). This will be not least because its strategies will be consistent and will be supported by its staff at all levels. What is a worthwhile vision is, however, usually open to debate, indeed to considerable debate. It is not sufficient merely to say, as some do, that 'we want to maximise profit' or even that 'we want to invest in the customer relationship'. An effective mission statement must say something genuinely important about the organisation; and must explain why it is in business (and why it should be allowed to stay in business!).

In a report in the *Harvard Business Review* (July/August 1960), Theodore Levitt pointed out one shortcoming – which he memorably described as 'marketing myopia' – that most organisations defined their business perspectives too narrowly, typically based upon the technological processes that they employed (but, at best, upon internal factors). His view, which was enthusiastically seized upon by the more adventurous organisations, was that the link with the consumer, the 'customer franchise', was the most important element. As you will have gathered, this is also my own view. The corporate vision must, therefore, be defined in terms of the customer's needs and wants.

<hr>

Activity 7.3

What is the stated corporate mission of your own organisation? Does it say anything worthwhile? What do you think the real 'vision' is, if there is one?

How does your own group's vision of its future fit in with that spelled out in the corporate mission statement?

How do you get there?

This last step should simply explain what marketing strategy is to be adopted to move the organisation from its present position to its targeted one over the longer term. The strategies describe, in principle, the 'how': how the objectives will be achieved. This strategy statement can take the form of a purely verbal description of the strategic options that have been chosen. Alternatively, and perhaps more positively, it might include a structured list of the major options chosen. On the other hand, 'strategy' is too often a term used to allow the senior management to do what they want, regardless of reality, and without undue interference: 'It is the board which sets the strategy, not you; you are just responsible for the results!' It is used to dignify their hunches, and to deflect criticism when these are wrong.

The reality is, as I said at the beginning of this chapter, that strategy is simply made up of the broad decisions that enable you to get from where you are to where you want to be. To achieve this, you may wish to use some of the ideas contained in this book, but only those few that are genuinely relevant to your needs should be employed. This is a very different approach from that traditionally employed, where the techniques employed at each stage tend to be pre-specified by the 'experts' who have devised the planning process. Thus, for instance, the Boston Matrix will be used to persuade you that you must milk your cash cows until they are dead, and the PLC will, in any case, suggest they are probably already well on their way to that death. Not all of these gimmicks are totally ineffective, however. The most widely used, the SWOT analysis, seems to provide some comfort for most managers.

A SWOT analysis is a very popular device, and is often used as a framework for analysing the external environment. It groups some of the key pieces of information, which you might have unearthed in your investigations, into two main categories (internal factors and external) and then by their dual positive and negative aspects (Strengths and Opportunities, as the former aspects, with Weaknesses and Threats representing the latter).

The factors internal to the organisation, but relating to its strategies and position in relation to its competitors, may be viewed as strengths or weaknesses, depending upon their impact on the organisation's position (for they may represent a strength for one organisation but a weakness, in relative terms, for another). They may refer to a physical product or an intangible service, to promotional activities or to personnel, finance etc. The factors presented by the external environment and the competition may again be threats to one organisation but offer opportunities to another. They may include such matters as technological change, legislation, socio-cultural change etc., as well as changes in the marketplace or competitive position.

You should note, however, that no matter how popular it is and even if its use is justified, SWOT is just one aid to categorisation. It is not, as many organisations seem to think, the only technique. We would, however, strongly recommend that you think very carefully before using it, since it has major weaknesses. In particular, it tends to persuade companies to compile lists rather than think what is really important to their business. It also presents the resulting lists uncritically, without clear prioritisation, so that, for example, a large number of weak opportunities may appear to balance a few strong threats.

One aspect of strategy that is often overlooked is that of timing. It is often critical to determine exactly when is the best time for each element of the strategy to be implemented. Taking the right action at the wrong time can sometimes be almost as bad as taking the wrong action at the right time. Timing is, therefore, an essential part of any marketing plan; and should normally appear as a schedule of planned activities in the last section of the planning documents – and must be allowed for at this stage in the strategies themselves.

Having completed this crucial stage of the planning process, you will need to re-check the feasibility of your objectives and strategies in terms of the market share, sales, costs, profits etc. that these demand in practice. As in the rest of the marketing discipline, you will need to employ judgement, experience, market research or anything else that helps you to look at your conclusions from all possible angles.

Activity 7.4

If you can, critically examine your organisation's strategy. How effective do you think it is? You may want to use SWOT analysis as a framework; but, please remember, do not get addicted to this approach (and remember its real limitations).

Do the same for your own group.

What action?

Finally, we need to positively *do* something! The shorter-term (more certain) elements of the strategies need to be translated into the necessary actions (and related timescales). Ideally, the plan should also contain space for the entry of actual results measured against these targets, since this will emphasise the true role of the plan and its relationship to the subsequent monitoring. The amount of information on the page may, however, demand a very small font size!

Such a marketing plan, as you will now realise, should be contained in just a few pages, although related appendices may be much longer. The acid test is how short it is. Longer than ten pages may mean that it is not read. It is also, within these important space constraints, free-form. The content of each section is dictated solely by what is important to the organisation at that time, in accordance with the philosophy we have been following throughout the book.

Activity 7.5

If you can get a copy of your organisation's marketing plan, critically examine it in terms of what you have learned from this book. Try to sketch out the changes you think should be made to it.

Make a (simpler) version for your own group.

➡ INCREMENTAL STRATEGY IN PRACTICE

Such rational decision making is, even once a year, the exception rather than the rule. The reality is that much strategy is set incrementally by small decisions taken, as the need arises, throughout a year. Thus, something happens in the market-place and you have to react immediately; and you simply don't have the time to change the strategy – or even consult it! These small decisions then accumulate until they ultimately dictate the overall strategy when this comes to be formalised, in written form, at the end of the year. The importance of this concept emerges in three contexts. The first is that managers moving into the rational phase of the annual planning process need to be aware of the limitations posed by the legacy of incremental decisions that have built up since the last annual exercise. The second is that an understanding of this process helps you to put such incremental decision making into perspective. Thirdly and most important of all, it alerts you to the fact that it is happening – all the time.

Take the example of positioning. As and when position drift is detected, the wise brand manager will react immediately; he or she will recognise that such response cannot wait for the annual plan. If the brand manager understands the implications of incremental strategies, however, he or she will inject some of the rational thinking that is supposed to lie at the heart of the annual planning process – the key to such incrementalism is, indeed, that it is still a logical process. In this way, it can be just as rational as the traditional process. It is not the same as the random decision making that infects many organisations. Because it recognises the reality that decisions are driven by real events rather than a theoretical planning process, it may indeed be rather more effective, but the decisions take place almost randomly throughout the year rather than tidily during the annual planning process.

One of the hidden implications of the above processes, which reflects my own experiences of much of such decision making (and which is supported by significant amounts of research data), is that the making of strategy is a much more diffused process than most managers think. A less obvious implication still is that the process is not limited to senior management alone, as traditional theory would suggest. In practice, the process is spread through a number of layers of management, with different degrees of involvement, depending upon what particular incremental aspect of strategy is under review. This has major implications for some managers, who have not realised just how important was their own contribution.

Even though incrementalism is very different from the traditionally described theory, it is still a very rational approach to management, and one where the manager is still very much in control. Although this is much closer to reality than traditional theory, it still neglects one very important aspect, which is that a considerable amount of strategy emerges as a result of unpredictable changes in the environment rather than from rational control by management. This emergent strategy means that managers are forced to follow courses of action that they had not planned.

Emergent strategy

Here, the intended strategy, decided upon traditionally or incrementally, is overtaken by events in two main ways. One, which will probably be recognised by the organisation, is that of unrealised strategy, where it proves simply impossible to implement the chosen strategy in practice. Less obvious is the 'emergent strategy', which is decided by events in the external environment and thus forced upon the organisation. This may not necessarily be recognised in its totality by the organisation, since many of its implications may be hidden. As markets become more complex, however, such emergent strategies are becoming more common.

Many organisations see both unrealised and emergent strategies in terms of failure – they have been forced, usually by unpredictable events, to abandon their own strategy. There is, accordingly, a tendency for these unwelcome facts to be ignored until they are so obvious that they cannot be avoided. This is a major error. Such deviations must be recognised (probably through one or other form of environmental analysis, coupled with networking) as soon as possible so that the organisation can react in good time. Indeed, this is not a failure but – if handled properly – a success.

Thus, a much more powerful approach is to seize positively upon these deviations as the basis for future developments. What needs to be recognised is that emergent strategies are the most powerful strategies of all – since they must, by definition, be derived from the needs of the market. Where even successful deliberate strategies may not ideally match market needs, emergent strategies are, almost by definition, likely to be vigorous ones.

There are two main approaches to capitalising on such emergent strategies. The first of these, favoured in the West, is the 'umbrella strategy'. This is a form of very positive delegation, in that the overall strategies (the umbrella) are very general in nature and this allows the lower-level managers, who are closest to the external environment, the freedom to react to emergent changes.

A much more direct, and hence even more powerful, approach is that favoured by the Japanese corporations. They integrate emergent strategies with their own. Indeed, it is arguable that, in terms of marketing, they use emergent strategies to a large extent *instead* of their own deliberate strategies. This is evidenced as much by an attitude of mind as by any other feature. They deliberately go out to look for the symptoms of such emergent trends, which can be detected in the performance of their own products. More than that, though, they often deliberately launch a range of products, rather than a single one, to see which is the most successful. It is almost as if they deliberately seek out the emergent strategies by offering the best environment for them to develop – the very reverse of the Western approach which seeks to avoid it!

The Japanese then go on to build on these emergent strategies with a number of very effective tools, most of which are designed to overcome the major problem that accompanies emergent strategies, namely that they emerge on the scene much later than deliberate ones (and are likely to be visible to all the competitors at the same time) so that time is of the essence in revising strategy. Thus, time-management techniques (including parallel development along with flexible and just-in-time manufacturing), which have been developed to a fine art by the Japanese, offer that nation and others like it a significant competitive advantage in handling such emergent strategies.

Activity 7.6

How does your organisation handle incremental decisions? Does it recognise their impact?

How does it handle emergent strategies? Does it capitalise on them, or does it treat them as failures of planning?

How does your own group recognise, and manage, the incremental (and emergent) changes facing it?

➡ **THE VALUE OF THE PLANNING PROCESS**

Despite the many shortcomings in practice, we should not dismiss the production of a marketing plan as too flawed to use. There are many different forms that are recommended for such plans, and you will find some of these in my own books, but all that is necessary is that you record – as briefly as possible – what are your key decisions as to how you will achieve your objectives, in terms of strategy and, in particular, in terms of positive actions.

At the same time, you should recognise that almost nobody will then read the plan! But, though the plan itself may not be as central to marketing actions as theorists would like, its production still produces some important benefits, as follows:

- **Review**. The process forces a full review of *all* the marketing factors, not just those that are currently the focus of attention, albeit that the review only occurs once a year.

- **Agreement**. The process acts as a positive stimulus to involvement of a wide range of personnel in the strategic decision making, and then as a framework for generating formal agreement amongst them.

- **Communication**. The output, the marketing plan itself, can be an especially useful vehicle for communicating the organisation's marketing intentions to the wider community (amongst its staff).

At this stage there may be, if the process is well managed, considerable benefit to be gained from the active involvement of a wide range of staff. This must, as a matter of principle, include all the managers who will be asked to implement it, but it should also be extended to the largest possible number of other employees. Involvement in the planning of your own future is highly motivational at all levels of staff and management – and exclusion from the process leads to frustration and fear.

The planning review process should, if properly managed, pose a suitably stimulating challenge to the embedded wisdom; especially where decisions taken on the spur of the moment – with little thought – have subsequently been incorporated as a strategy that is never then challenged (regardless of whether it is right or wrong). This debate should be as wide-ranging as possible. Nothing should be exempt from scrutiny, and no idea should be dismissed until fully considered. The range of creativity tools, such as brainstorming, can also be brought into play. It is the one chance, during the year, to think the unthinkable.

Probably the most productive part of the whole process, though, is the opportunity to gain a shared understanding of what the marketing plan means, although the fact that it has been 'published' in no way guarantees that it is then understood by the recipients. By positively involving them in its production, you best ensure that they will be firmly committed to its implementation. This process is probably best accomplished in an extended meeting away from the pressure of day-to-day business; and this will inevitably cover far more than is eventually enshrined in the plan itself. It is this shared 'flavour' that will inform the actions of those involved over the succeeding year – and it is the most potent outcome of this part of the process.

Activity 7.7

Who is involved in the planning processes of your own organisation? Are you yourself involved? If not, why not?

Whom do you involve in the planning processes of your own group? Do you use them to motivate your own staff?

➡ COMPETITION

One element of marketing that has only been dealt with incidentally so far is that of how the marketer competes against other manufacturers or service providers in the market. Competition is a major factor in most markets, and hence in most marketing activities. Above all, it should be remembered that the characteristics of the key product (or service) are not seen as absolute, in isolation, by the customers; rather they are seen as relative, in comparison with the other suppliers' offerings. The marketer must know, therefore, what his offering's relative performance is on all fronts.

Led by Michael Porter, the marketing developments of the 1980s (and indeed those of overall corporate strategy) were dominated by competitive policy. This focus remedied the previous neglect of the subject; but there was a degree of overreaction, to the extent that for some companies – and some governments – competitive policy is now too often seen as more important than all other aspects of marketing, including the customer!

According to the theory developed in this field, the first level of understanding of the competitive environment is that of the 'industry' (in its broadest sense, be it frozen foods or health service provision) within which the organisation operates. Thus, the 'character' of that industry is supposed largely to determine the competitive activities taking place within it, and the profits of most of the participants.

The larger the market, the more attractive it will generally be to new entrants, and the more important it may become. On the other hand, the larger the market, the more likely it will be that it will be segmented. It might also seem that the greater the number of organisations in a market, the more competitive it might be, and this is generally true – if the brands are of roughly the same size. But the level of competition may also be related to the pattern of concentration of the overall business into the hands of the major players: clearly, a monopoly will significantly reduce competitive forces! The most stable, and profitable, market (apart from a pure monopoly) is usually that with one or two dominant brands and a few smaller brands.

In any case, in order to avoid competition, the most sophisticated marketers will aim to differentiate their product or service from the others in the market. In general, the more that products or services are differentiated, the less direct will be the competition.

It is often considered, by those most influenced by competition theory, that economies of scale are the main features of any market. The theory is that the greater the economies of scale, the greater will be the benefits coming to those with large shares of the market and hence the greater the competition to achieve such larger shares. Such economies of scale may come about because larger plants are more efficient to run, and cost relatively little per unit of output to build. Or they may come about because there are overhead costs that cannot be avoided, even by the smaller organisations, but which can be spread over larger volumes by the bigger players. Or they may come about because of 'learning effects', in this case related to accumulated volume: the more that is produced, the more the manufacturer learns – finding ever more efficient ways of production. All of these effects tend to increase competition by offering incentives to 'buy' market share in order to become the lowest-cost producer.

But there can be less obvious barriers raised against new entrants. It has long been the case that sitting tenants in large markets have managed to persuade government, paradoxically often as a response to complaints of cartels dominating the market, to enact legislation to govern the competitive behaviour of the main players, even if that was against the intention of the original government intervention. Alternatively, if the distribution channels can be denied to competitors, then competition can be limited. It is rare for single products to achieve this, although the brewers and the oil companies with their 'tied' outlets have achieved something close to this. Supermarket chains, however, will often only stock the two leading brands, thus effectively limiting serious competition to those two brands.

Perhaps the most sensitive indicator of price competition is the degree of overcapacity. Beware those markets, particularly those with economies of scale, where there is a significant amount of spare capacity. If it exists, you can be sure that everyone will be focusing on sales (and hence production) levels, almost regardless of price; and – as we have seen in Chapter 4 – that almost inevitably leads to low, commodity-based, prices.

Activity 7.8

What, in your opinion, determines competitive strategies in your industry?

Competitive responses

In practice, in most stable markets, the best indicator of competitive strategies is simple history – what has happened before. The previous reactions of competitors will to a large extent indicate what the new competitive moves will be, particularly in terms of the reactions to new entrants.

Even so, probably the most important, but often neglected, analysis is the determination of how each of the competitors may respond to future changes. There are four main categories of possible response:

- **Non-response (or slow response)**. It may be that a competitor responding in this manner is in such a strong position that it does not see the need to respond directly to any changes in the environment. Conversely, the competitor may be in a particularly *weak* position, and cannot resource any reaction.

- **Fast response**. There are a few organisations that have a policy of immediate and substantial response (often a deliberate overkill) – as much as a deterrent to future challengers as to the current threat. This strategy is usually the most effective over the longer term – and the most cost-effective, since the sooner the threat is removed, the sooner high profits can be generated again.

- **Focused response**. Some competitors will only respond to certain types of challenge (typically on price), either refusing to accept or simply not recognising other forms of challenge (particularly those in the form of product development).

- **Unpredictable response**. This is the most difficult response to deal with, and is from those organisations whose responses cannot be predicted at all!

Activity 7.9

What is the form of your organisation's normal competitive response, and those of its competitors?

➡ STRATEGY: A FOOTNOTE

As we have seen, there are many suggestions – not least in many books – as to how you should develop your strategy and just as many suggestions – freely given, uninfluenced by the facts of your situation – as to what must be the *ideal* strategy. I will simply suggest that the perfect strategy for your own organisation will be the unique one that specifically matches your needs. The heart of the matter is quite simply the question, 'How will you get from where you now are to where you want to be?' *Only you can decide what the answer is.*

Your response should be based largely upon your common sense rather than any high-flown theories, but please remember to invest in your long-term survival. This latter is, as we shall see in the final chapter, a crucial element of marketing, and usually means investing in the relationship with your customers. Indeed, it always makes sense to have dialogue with those customers, but (I repeat) it would be both arrogant and foolish of me, or any other marketing academic, to predict exactly what might emerge from that dialogue!

Chapter 8
Long-range marketing

As we saw in the previous chapter, typical approaches to marketing strategy focus on a relatively short-term time frame – for example, through the use of matrices the impact of current actions may be balanced, or derived from existing forces such as competitive pressures, or (stressing the short-term nature of decisions) derived from incremental and emergent strategies. Even so, it is often claimed that the widely reported problems of short-termism in corporate strategy come about not because the philosophy is incorrect but because of management shortcomings.

On the other hand, with more than five years of direct experience (including teaching several thousand MBA students, and advising a range of clients) backed by research amongst more than a thousand organisations, I have come to the conclusion that the main problems for most organisations are not the result of incompetent management but are caused by a confusion of objectives. Thus, I now believe that there should be at least two quite separate processes at work in organisations, rather than the one traditionally recommended. There is, of course, the conventional corporate strategy process, optimising performance in the shorter term, which we all know about. But there should also be a *separate*, presently well hidden, process of producing 'robust strategies' that underpin survival over the longer term.

That there are, or should be, these two quite distinct legs to the strategy process – whether hidden or not – is demonstrated by the table in Figure 8.1, which clearly establishes the significant differences between them. Indeed, the two sets of strategies should have very different objectives. Marketing strategy, as well as corporate strategy is quintessentially about optimising current performance, which requires that you find the single short-term solution that will deliver the optimal (internal) performance most effectively to which members of the organisation can be persuaded to commit themselves. The classic example demands the single objective of producing the highest bottom-line profit for the current year. 'Robust' strategies, on the other hand, are, above all, about survival in the longer term; ensuring that all the potential threats are covered. They demand that multiple, and often divergent, objectives are met in order to exploit the potential emerging from changes in the (external) environment, and especially to guard against the whole range of threats that might endanger survival in the longer term, with the aim of understanding what these might be.

In terms of basic characteristics, marketing (corporate) strategy is usually supposed to follow a rational approach (often deductive,

	Marketing/Corporate Strategy	Robust Strategies
OBJECTIVES	optimising performance	ensuring survival
CHARACTERISTICS	short-term, single-focus	long-term, divergent-coverage
OUTCOMES	effectiveness commitment	comprehensiveness understanding
RECIPIENTS OF BENEFITS	individual profiteers	stakeholder communities

Figure 8.1: Strategy differences

arguing from the general to the particular), whereas robust strategies are evolutionary in nature and best approached inductively (working from the specific pieces of evidence to some general conclusions).

It should be clear, therefore, that there may be considerable tension between these two forms of strategy, not least because they have very different objectives aimed at producing potentially very different outcomes to satisfy very different groups of stakeholders!

Activity 8.1

Try out this comparison for your own organisation.

➡ DIFFERENT STAKEHOLDERS

Let me expand upon this last point. In the modern corporation, the individual 'shareholders' are no longer involved in managing the company themselves. Indeed, their investment in it may be as fleeting as a millisecond, as computers trade the shares on the electronic stockmarkets around the world. Understandably, therefore, their focus is only on the ephemeral performance of the share price, which may – in the very short term on which they single-mindedly concentrate – be more directly linked to stockmarket rumours than to the financial performance of the firm. The individual senior managers of the organisations, sometimes known as the 'fat cats' (the other group of 'insider' beneficiaries), *are* interested in financial performance; but again only in terms of the short-term results, for their own performance – and even more directly, their income – is often tied to the company's share price. As they are usually but a few years away from claiming their pension, they have every incentive to optimise the current results – on which that pension will be based – and to hell with the long term. Put in this context, it is obvious why both these sets of key actors demand that corporate strategy focuses on short-term financial performance. To put it crudely, neither group will be around when long-term strategy saves the company!

The various communities, though, hold a very different perspective. The employees of the organisation, most of whom are some way from retirement, have a very direct interest in the *long-term* survival of the organisation, for on this depends their own survival. Even though many of them will, in time, change to jobs with other organisations, they still want the safety net of a future in their current position. The other communities of stakeholders, from suppliers and customers through to the local communities that are dependent upon the organisation, have similar requirements that look for long-term survival of the organisation. With governments increasingly recognising the right of these communities to participate in the management of organisations, it is likely that such longer-term viewpoints may eventually prevail – and robust strategies will finally come into their own!

Activity 8.2

Does a conflict of interest between short- and long-term aims exist (or potentially exist) within your own organisation? If so, how can it be reconciled?

➡ A LONG-RANGE MARKETING PLAN

I believe that the best answer to reconciling the differences between these two aspects of strategy is simply to separate the two processes, which is the opposite of what is currently recommended. In view of the fact that it deals almost exclusively with forces coming from outside the organisation, which would normally be incorporated into its 'marketing' strategy, we call this process 'long-range marketing'. This philosophy is formally encapsulated in the production of a long-range marketing plan which, much like the conventional (short-term) marketing plan, ultimately feeds into the corporate plan. This is the 'long-range planning' process that I now teach my OU students and recommend for my consultancy clients, with some success in at least raising their awareness of long-term trends.

Environmental analysis (scanning)

Much as conventional marketing is based upon sound marketing research, long-range marketing demands the best possible environmental analysis; often referred to as 'scanning'. This is a very wide-ranging activity, covering much more ground than traditional market research. Indeed, in its broadest sense it encompasses all those activities that the organisation uses, formally and informally, to keep abreast of those changes in the external environment that will affect its future. At its widest, it can include all the factual (news and documentary) material to be seen on television or read in the newspapers and periodicals! In this widest sense, scanning is defined as a general exposure to information where there is no specific purpose in mind (with the possible exception of exploration). It is characterised by a general unawareness as to what issues might be raised. The sources of information are many and varied, the amounts are relatively great, and the screening is generally coarse, only alerting someone to the fact that something has changed. This compares with market research, where there is a deliberate effort to seek out specific information.

You can see why such scanning is not just difficult but also potentially very expensive. In practice, an organisation can focus on only a small part of the information that keeps pouring in upon it from its environment. As we have seen, the ultimate incentive for investing the necessary time and resources in these processes is a realisation of just how important these activities may be to preserving the long-term future of the organisation.

Possibly the simplest, and best, practical advice in relation to scanning is to cultivate a deep, on-going, curiosity about the external world, coupled with an ability to recognise which signals, from amongst the mass of data that every new day brings, are relevant – and important – to the future of the organisation. Indeed, in practice, I have found that almost all the participants in the OU's successful long-range marketing programmes have used general reading as the main source of their analysis, combined with the more specific information they receive from their industry and the specialist press that they read as a normal part of their work. Indeed, it has to be noted that the type of information required for the scenarios subsequently set out here is most probably that which the participants have *already* assimilated. They need to bring to the scenario process no more than their existing knowledge.

In addition, there seems to be no special expertise involved in detecting significant shifts in the environment. Indeed, I have found that the best approach is to analyse the external environment as a team. If nothing else, this extends the coverage of the scanning process, but it also seems to go much further in amplifying the early signs of change and in developing understanding, as the six to eight team members interact with each other and compare notes as the process develops.

Activity 8.3

Briefly undertake an environmental analysis of those parts of the external environment that will most impact the future of your organisation.

Do the same for your own group, perhaps involving other members of your group in this activity.

Scenario forecasting

The subsequent 'formal' planning processes start with scenario forecasting, although in a much simpler form than the approaches that were more usually adopted in the past. Our own version at the Open University, using relatively simple scenarios, comprises five main steps:

1. Decide on the drivers for change, namely what the forces are that will decide the long-term future of your organisation.
2. Cluster the drivers together into groups that are easier to handle but that still make sense.
3. Reduce these groups to no more than nine mini-scenarios, again so that these are easier to handle.
4. Reduce the list to two scenarios – but only because more than this number is likely to confuse those using them.
5. Write the scenarios, as reports about two alternative futures.

The whole process is now simple enough that it can be undertaken in as little as half a day, with a management team using little more than brief *aides-mémoires* to facilitate their thinking. Even so, this is a critical aspect of the long-range planning process since only if the key turning points are identified in these scenarios will the (robust) strategies developed in response be valid.

Thus, the first stage of our scenario forecasting, namely deciding the drivers for change, should be to examine the results of the environmental analysis to determine which are the most important factors that will decide the nature of the future environment within which the organisation will operate. In reality, as formal scanning is rarely undertaken and the participants should all have been exposed to a wide range of analytical inputs as part of their day-to-day work, their existing knowledge proves quite sufficient for them to productively engage in the debate and produce meaningful results.

As hinted at above, the simple technique that my colleagues and I have come to recommend requires only a conference room with a bare wall and copious supplies of 3M Post-It Notes™. The six to eight people taking part in the scenario group are simply asked to identify the most important drivers for (global) change, which are then written on the Notes and placed on the wall.

The next step is to link these drivers together to provide a meaningful framework for the future. This is where managers' intuition – their ability to make sense of complex patterns of 'soft' data that more rigorous analysis would be unable to handle – plays an important role. Participants are asked to try and arrange the drivers into groups that seem to make sense to them. Then these are merged into no more than nine larger groupings the 'mini-scenarios' mentioned in step 3 of the five-point list above.

In the final stage, that of reducing the groupings to just two scenarios, the group member are, in the first instance, encouraged to find a theme – and in particular a title – for each of the two scenarios. These themes should, as far as possible, encapsulate the main trends that have been unearthed. I have found it best to talk about the 'flavour' of the future for their industry. They then allocate, again as far as possible, the clusters (or mini-scenarios) to each of these alternative scenarios (themes) in order to create the final scenarios. This process is very different from that used by the most sophisticated forecasters. But it does produce results, and results that are good enough to use as input to a long-range marketing plan.

Try the process just described on your own group. Do not take it too seriously, but do it primarily for the sake of understanding what is involved. You should nevertheless still find the outcome enlightening.

With the aim of reducing the rest of the long-range marketing process to the bare minimum, there are just five further simple steps to producing that long-range marketing plan, as set out hereafter.

Isolate the turning points

The starting point of the plan itself must be a definitive statement of what has emerged from the scenario work. Ideally, this should be a formal 'map' of some kind, giving the issues, the 'turning points', which will decide the long-term future of your organisation and perhaps even its very survival. This is the step that defeats most organisations. If you do not recognise what factors will determine your fate, then you will not be able to create the most effective robust strategies to address them.

The first requirement, here, is to identify which are the key issues that the robust strategies should address. This is, once more, a process of focusing on the key factors that must be addressed, in the context of limited resources. The main emphasis in this process is, therefore, on *prioritisation*: deciding which factors are crucial to the future of the organisation, matters of life and death, and which are relatively less important. A lesser dimension in this process will also be that of judging the likelihood of a given turning point actually occurring – but it should be noted that even a relatively unlikely event will need to be considered if its impacts could be central to the future development of the organisation.

This is also probably best undertaken as a group process. My experience suggests that most groups move, at this stage, from the use of Post-It Notes™ (which are the staple diet of our scenario work) to use of more mundane flip-charts or white boards to communicate and record their decisions.

Decide the robust strategies

Despite coming near the end, this stage is at the heart of the whole process. What is needed is a set of strategies, known as 'robust' strategies, to protect against (or to capitalise on) what has emerged from the previous steps in terms of effectively addressing the key turning points. In practice, it often proves to be easier than the earlier stages since (as is often the case) asking the right question is often harder than producing the most effective answer.

The best format for this part of the process towards a long-range marketing plan may just be a simple two-column table, with the key turning points in the left-hand column and the matching robust strategies in the right-hand one.

Activity 8.5

Extend your group's work to these further steps.

Test against corporate strategy

This step is the one that definitively separates the new approach from the traditional one. It is however, a step that requires a degree of self-confidence! It involves taking these (long-term) robust strategies and mapping them onto the (short-term) corporate strategy that already exists (or is in the process of emerging from other parts of the strategy process). Exactly what form this comparison takes will depend upon what form you have adopted for presenting these strategies. The essence, however, is that each robust-onto-corporate mapping should involve a comparison, statement by statement, with the strategy descriptions. Ideally, this should again be in the form of a simple table, with just two columns, one for each side of the comparison.

Decide strategic changes

Emerging directly from that step will be a clear definition of the divergences, if any, between the two types of strategy. This will, therefore, immediately highlight the nature of any change to be made. These should then be addressed, again statement by statement, in terms of the changes that should accordingly be made in the overall corporate strategy statement, even if the decision is to do nothing! The simplest way to record these changes is to add them as a third column to the table used in the preceding step.

Translate into action

The final stage of any planning process should always be to *do* something! It may be that the action is positively to incorporate these changes into the overall corporate plan. In this case, a single sentence, stating that this has happened may be enough – although to reassure yourself, at least, that this has indeed happened, you may want to incorporate a brief statement of what real changes have taken place.

The more thorough alternative is to produce a separate action plan where the shorter-term (more certain) elements of the revised strategy are translated into the necessary actions (and related timescales). Again, this may be in the form of a table describing the key activities in terms of the most relevant parameters. Their prioritisation levels and resource requirements should be listed, at least, along with their target outcomes and times. Allowing for updating in this way emphasises the true role of the long-range marketing plan and its relationship to the subsequent monitoring.

Activity 8.6

Finally, complete your group exercise by extending it through to the final steps to the action plan.

What have you learned about the long-term future of your group from this exercise?

➡ GENERIC ROBUST STRATEGIES

The process can pose problems for management. For instance, they might be asked to *definitely* reduce short-term profits in order to safeguard against *possible* problems in the longer-term (which might occur when they have retired – on a pension linked to those *short-term* profits!). Fortunately, in practice the problem is usually not as acute as it might be expected to be. Thus, in my experience – and despite the seeming contradictions – the two types of strategy typically converge on much the same approach. Indeed, the two processes most often converge on a range of 'generic' long-term strategies, most typically on strategies that are in any case justifiable as sound marketing practice (for example, building relationships with customers, which was stressed in the earlier part of the book) and which prove equally effective in both the shorter and longer term.

Our work at the Open University has shown that there may be a range of traditional investments, typically in intangibles, that can go some way to underwriting the long-term survival of most organisations regardless of what the future developments are. We refer to these as 'generic' robust strategies. It should be noted that these are quite different from Michael Porter's generic strategies, which relate to the province of (shorter-term) corporate strategies.

In general, the main investments in this category relate to the relationships built up (i.e. invested in) with the main groups of stakeholders. In essence, the benefit of such investment is to create the goodwill that allows any organisation the breathing space necessary for it to regroup – for instance carrying through a programme of creative imitation – in the face of changes that would otherwise be cataclysmic. Of course, the organisation has to have sufficient speed of reaction to overcome the problems before the goodwill runs out, but the goodwill itself is what allows the possibility of recovery. Indeed, the best solution for creating the degree of flexibility needed is to engender a parallel sense of goodwill amongst your own staff – another key set of stakeholders – exactly as I explained in Chapter 7 in the section on 'inner marketing'.

Activity 8.7

How does your organisation stand in relation to these two groups of
stakeholders (customers and employees)? Does it have the necessary goodwill to underwrite its long-term survival?

➡ CONVERGENCE OF STRATEGIES

Even if the robust strategies and the corporate strategy prove to be
almost identical, the process of establishing what the robust
strategies might be is not just worthwhile but *necessary*. Without
undertaking that work, it is impossible to see whether there are any
hidden conflicts between the two. It may be more comfortable to
remain in ignorance, but in terms of survival it is much better to
know about any longer-term problems that you may be creating
for yourself in this way. More likely, there will only be minor
changes needed to ensure an even more secure long-term future.
Despite any irrational fears, and with the knowledge that – in most
cases – the long- and short-term strategies complement each other,
you will gain the additional confidence positively to reinforce your
short-term strategies.

Generally speaking, therefore, the impact of undertaking a
separate identification of robust strategies is not a major revision of
corporate strategy. In the relatively few cases where that *is* needed,
the robust strategies clearly need to become the dominant part of
the whole planning process. In general, though, it means the
development of a new prioritisation of existing strategy, with the
emphasis subtly shifted to allow for the longer term in addition to
the shorter one.

➡ STEERING

We refer to the final part of the process, implementing the changes
that are found to be necessary, as 'steering', since it is analogous to
the way an aircraft's autopilot makes regular small changes to its
short-term heading (the corporate strategy) in order to reach its
ultimate destination (the robust strategies).

Even so, the techniques underpinning the long-range marketing planning processes are different from those more conventionally adopted, Not least, they are more open-ended than prescriptive. The starting point is more typically a blank sheet of paper than one of the matrices recommended for shorter-term planning. In addition, as might perhaps be expected in view of the long timescales, they place much greater emphasis on investment. Thus, for instance, most marketing promotion such as advertising and PR, can be seen in this context as an investment in the longer term – be it in brand position or customer relationships – rather than a current cost.

In this way, we have found that, simply by separating out the longer-term robust strategies from the shorter-term corporate strategy in a formal long-range marketing plan, organisations are better able to take account of the longer term, avoiding the problems that can arise from the short-termism generated by the pressures currently facing managements. In any case, if they follow sound marketing practices, the price they might have to pay in terms of short-term steering is usually small, and the long-term benefits – not least continued survival – may be great.

Activity 8.8

What steering is needed to gently redirect your own group towards the longer-term robust strategies that you have developed, without unduly affecting its short-term performance?

➡ THE INVESTMENT MULTIPLIER

This brings us nicely to the final reminder of the most important aspect of marketing, which has been stressed throughout the book but which is still not widely recognised. This is the *investment over time*. In the earlier chapters, we saw that the most successful brands have very long lives. The difference in philosophy that this leads to is best evidenced by my preferred terminology, in the context of new products, of 'runners' rather than 'stars' (from the Boston Matrix) and 'winners' rather than 'cash cows'. I believe that winners – the brands which have proved themselves over time –

are to be cosseted (and not cash cows to be milked), and that runners – those still creating their places in the market – have to be carefully assessed (and not automatically presumed to be future stars). The history of a brand is the best indicator of its future: if it has been a high performer, it will continue to be so; if it has been long-lived, it will have a long life into the future too. What is more, a successful high-investment brand *multiplies* its already high return as a brand leader by having a longer life, over which the annual returns accumulate.

The brand investment over time is now usually the biggest investment any organisation makes. Yet it appears on very few balance sheets and is ignored by most managers – indeed, it is vandalised by many of them in their search for cost savings! Above all, though, this investment is in the relationship between the organisation (symbolised by the brand) and its customers. If this book has taught you nothing else, please remember just how important that relationship is!

Index